# This book belongs to:

# Look at Me!

Look into the mirror. Draw a self-portrait.
Print your name.

# Colours, Shapes and Sizes

Colour the crayons.

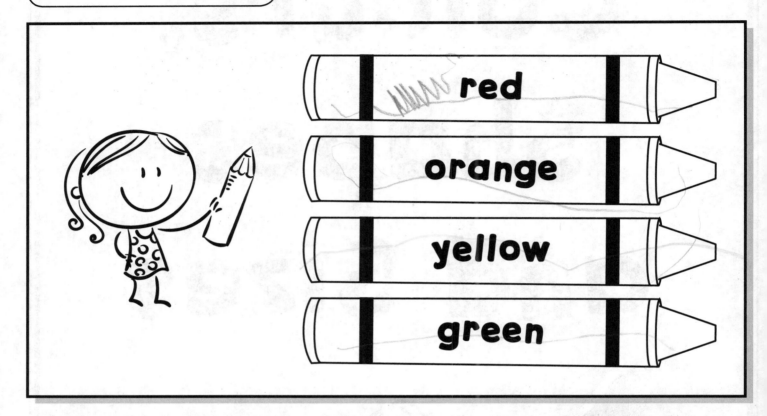

red

orange

yellow

green

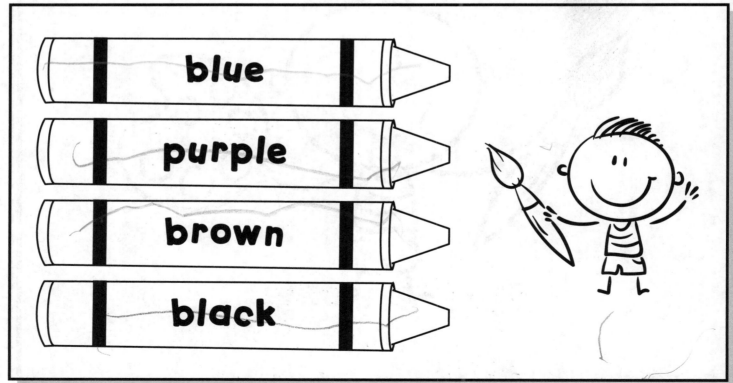

blue

purple

brown

black

# The Colour Red

Colour the pictures red.

red

stop sign

fire truck

apples

heart

Trace the word red.

red

Colour the pictures orange.

**carrot**

**pumpkin**

**orange**

**basketball**

Trace the word orange.

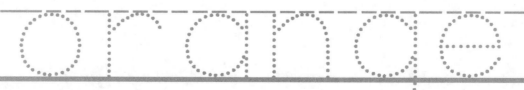

# The Colour Yellow

Colour the pictures yellow.

 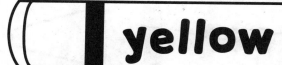 

**sun**

**bus**

**bananas**

**duck**

Trace the word yellow.

yellow

Colour the pictures green.

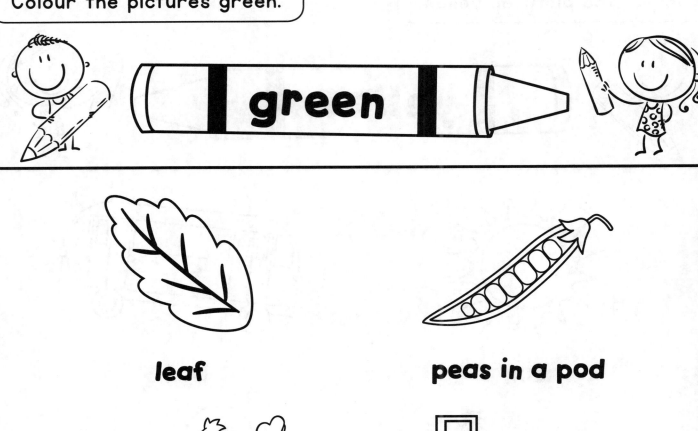

green

leaf

peas in a pod

alligator

truck

Trace the word green.

# The Colour Blue

Colour the pictures blue.

blue

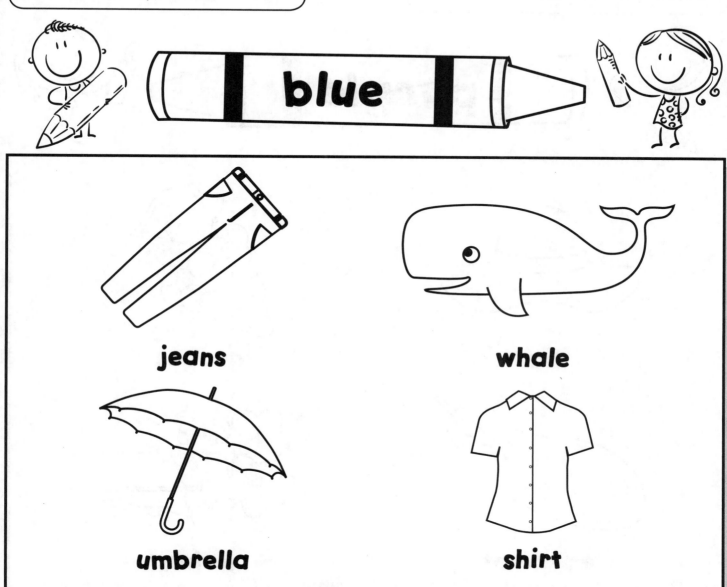

jeans

whale

umbrella

shirt

Trace the word blue.

blue

Colour the pictures purple.

purple

hat

grapes

eggplant

violets

Trace the word purple.

Colour the pictures black.

black

kettle

van

bat

sheep

Trace the word black.

black

Colour the pictures brown.

brown

mushroom

dog

potatoes

acorns

Trace the word brown.

brown

# Colouring Fun

Colour the picture.

# Looking at Shapes

A **circle** is a shape that is round. Trace the circles. Colour the circles.  red

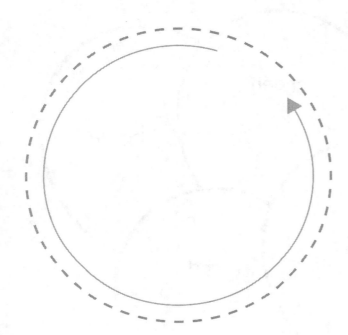

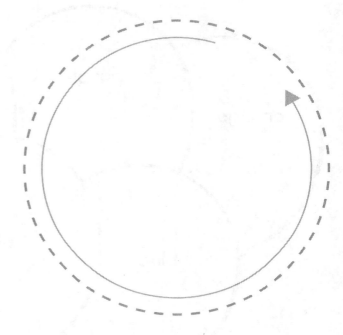

## Think about it!

You can find examples of circles all around you!

clock

wheel

A **square** is a shape with four equal sides. Trace the squares. Colour the squares. 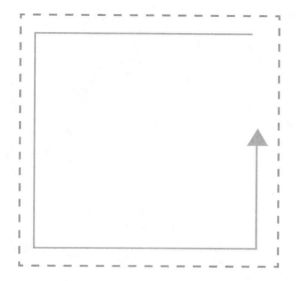 blue

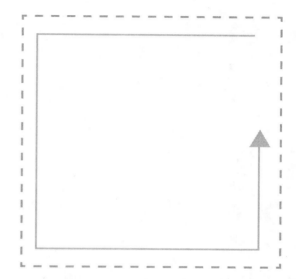

# Think about it!

You can find examples of squares all around you!

box

blocks

# Looking at Shapes

A **triangle** is a shape with three sides. Trace the triangles. Colour the triangles.  green

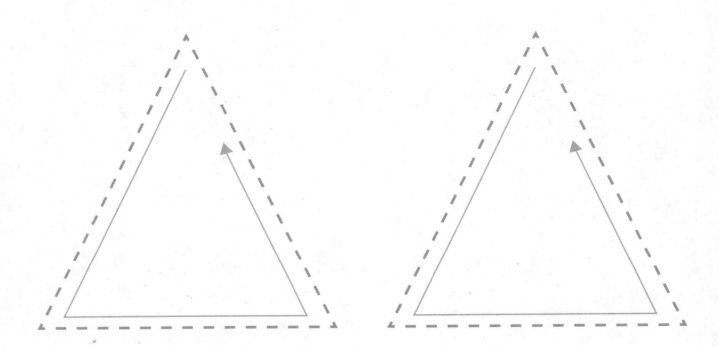

# Think about it!

You can find examples of triangles all around you!

pizza

ice cream cone

A **rectangle** is a shape with four sides. Trace the rectangles. Colour the rectangles.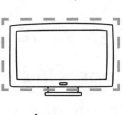

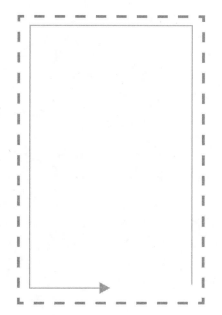

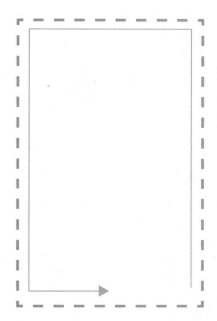

# Think about it!

You can find examples of rectangles all around you!

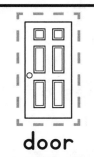

door          television

An **oval** is a shape. It is round, but a bit longer in one direction. Trace the ovals. Colour the ovals. | **purple** |

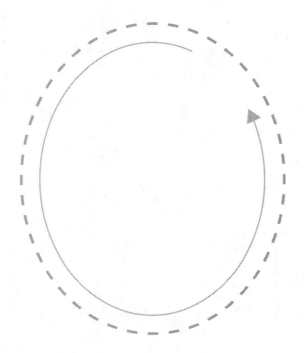 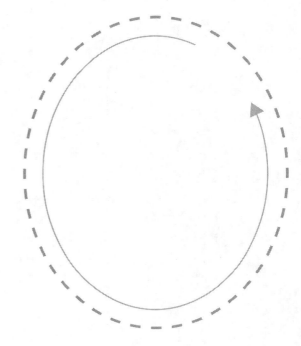

## Think about it!

You can find examples of ovals all around you!

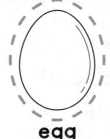

egg

light bulb

A **diamond** is a shape with four sides. Trace the diamonds. Colour the diamonds. ((| **yellow** |━▷

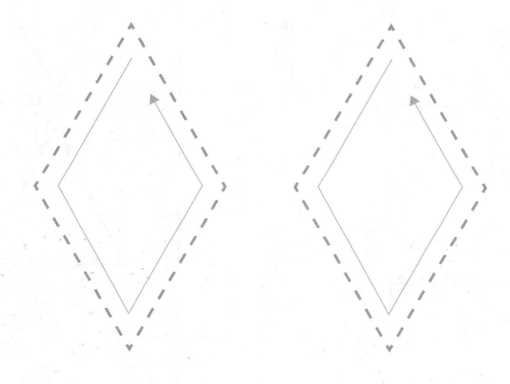

# Think about it!

You can find examples of diamonds all around you!

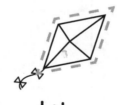

kite

road sign

# Shape Matching

Say the name of each shape out loud. Trace the shapes.
Draw a line to the matching shape. Colour the shapes.

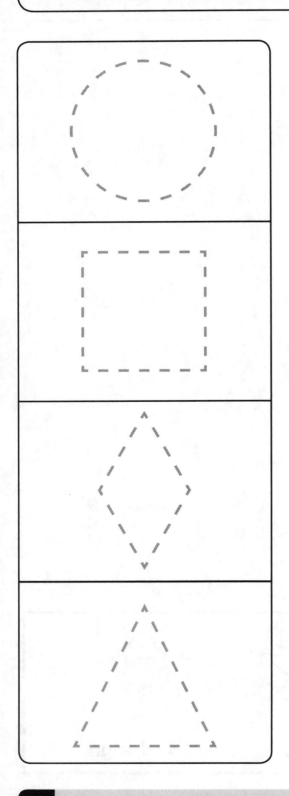

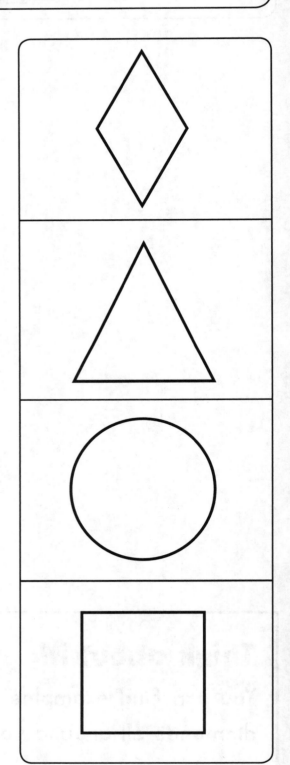

# Shape Matching

Say the name of each shape out loud. Trace the shapes.
Draw a line to the matching shape. Colour the shapes.

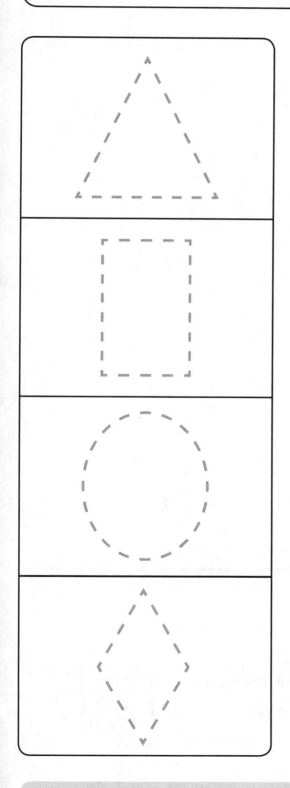

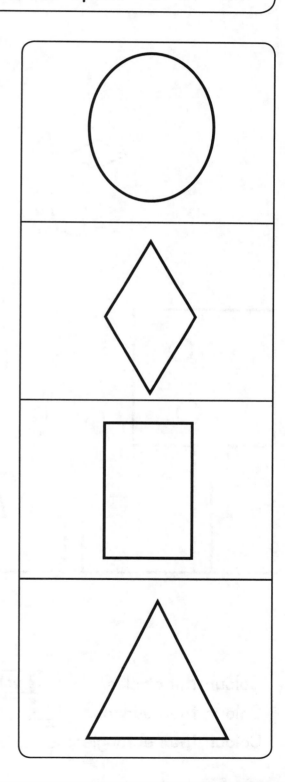

# Looking at Shapes

Trace all the shapes.
Use the colour key to colour the shapes.

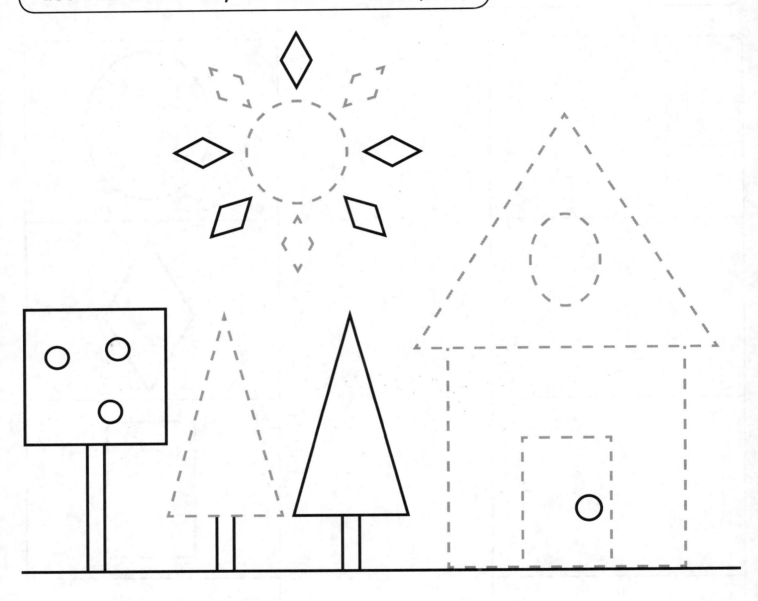

| Colour the circles. | yellow | Colour the triangles. | green |
| Colour the squares. | green | Colour the oval. | blue |
| Colour the rectangles. | brown | Colour the diamonds. | orange |

Trace all the shapes.

Use the colour key to colour the shapes.

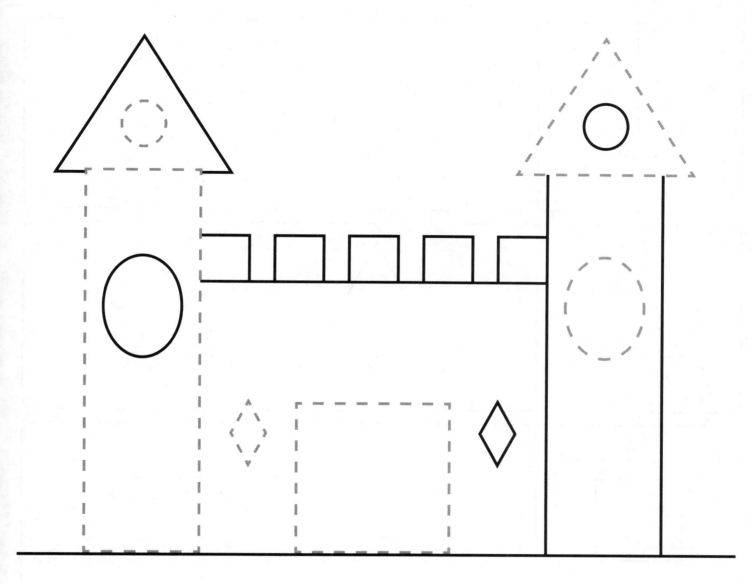

Colour the circles. red

Colour the squares. blue

Colour the rectangles. green

Colour the triangles. orange

Colour the ovals. yellow

Colour the diamonds. purple

# Looking at Same Size

Look at the first picture on each row.
Draw a circle around the shapes that are the **same**.

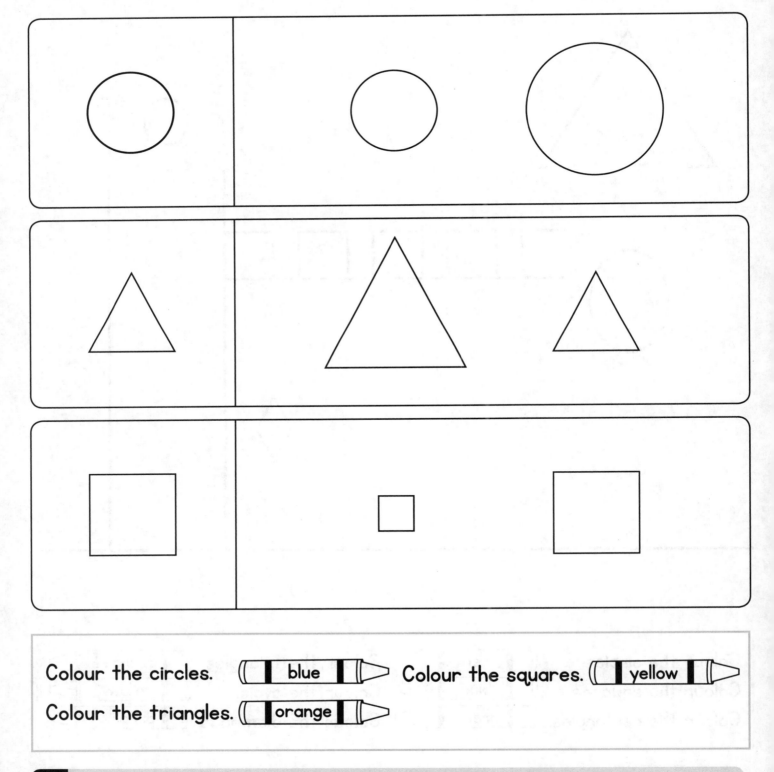

Colour the circles. [blue]    Colour the squares. [yellow]

Colour the triangles. [orange]

Look at the first picture on each row.
Draw a circle around the shapes that are **different**.

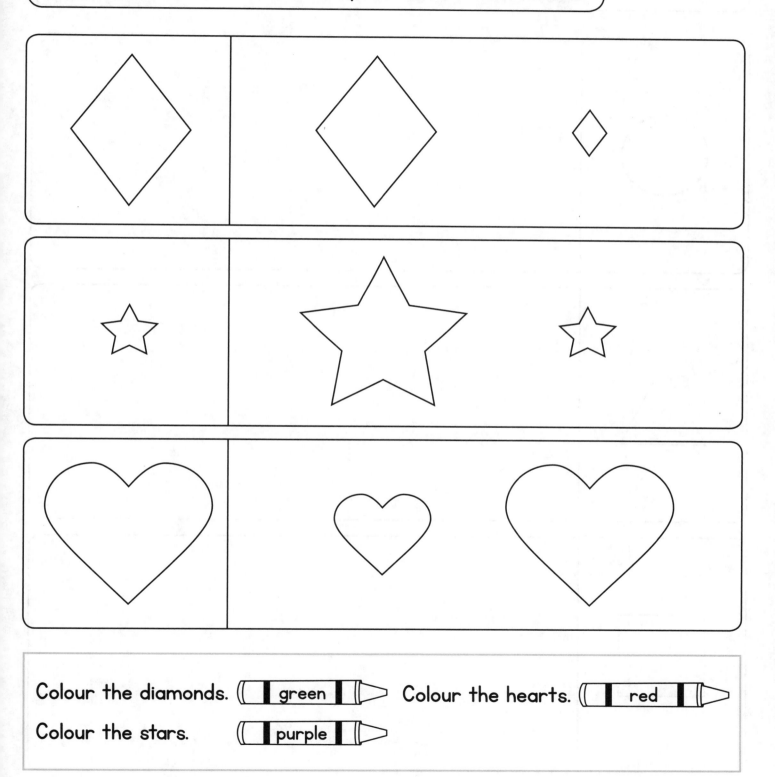

Colour the diamonds. green    Colour the hearts. red

Colour the stars. purple

# Drawing Bigger Shapes

Look at the shape in each row. Trace and then draw a **bigger** shape. Colour the shapes.

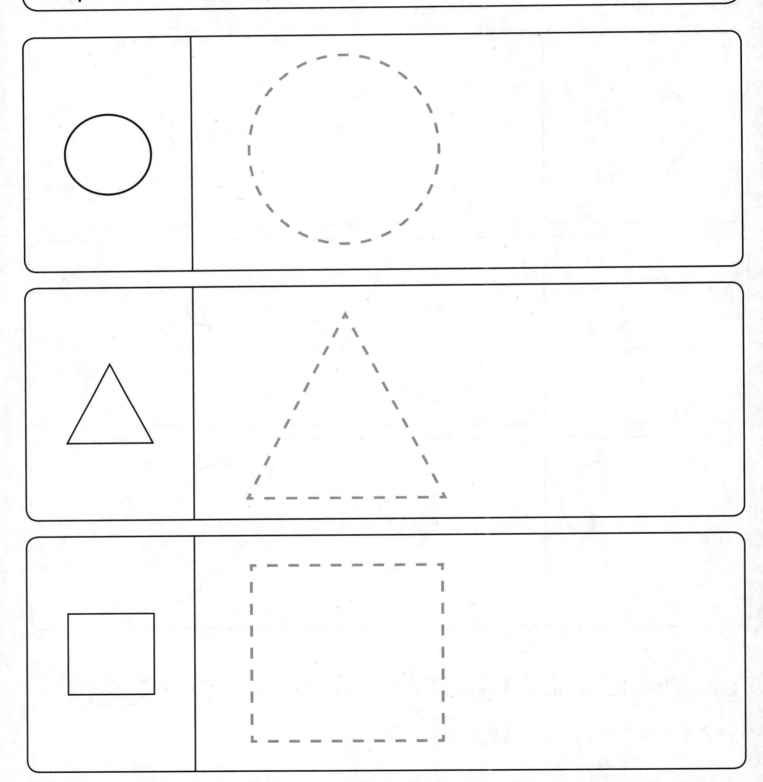

# Drawing Smaller Shapes

Look at the shape in each row. Trace and then draw a **smaller** shape. Colour the shapes.

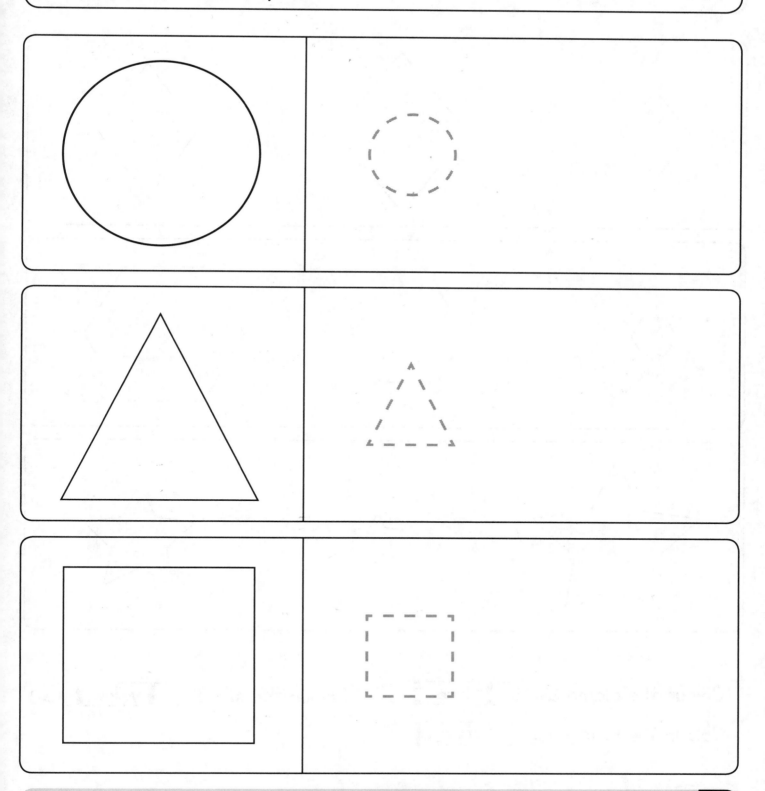

# Looking at the Biggest Size

Look at the shapes in each row.
Circle the **biggest** shape.

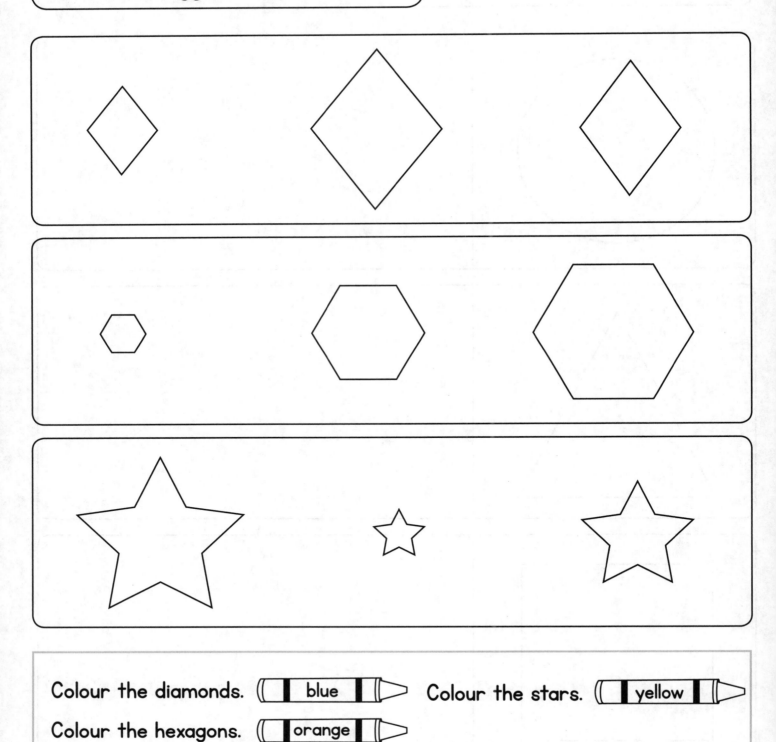

Colour the diamonds. blue    Colour the stars. yellow

Colour the hexagons. orange

Look at the shapes in each row.
Circle the **smallest** shape.

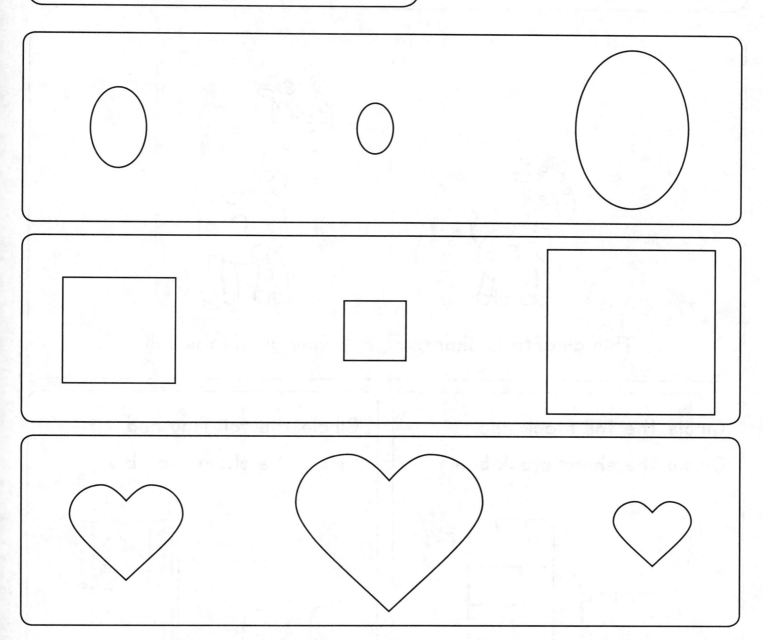

Colour the ovals. green   Colour the hearts. red

Colour the squares. purple

# Tall and Short

Draw a line from the correct word to the correct picture.
Colour the pictures.

Short

Tall

This giraffe is **short**.

This giraffe is **tall**.

Circle the **tall** stack red.
Circle the **short** stack blue.

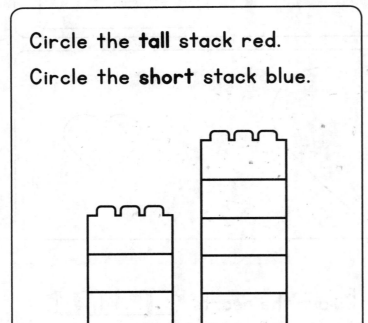

Circle the **tall** flag red.
Circle the **short** flag blue.

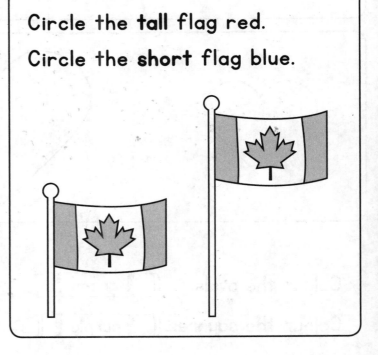

# Alphabet and Printing Skills

Trace the lines below.
Circle your best traced line.

## Think About it!

What bug do knights hate?
Dragonflies!

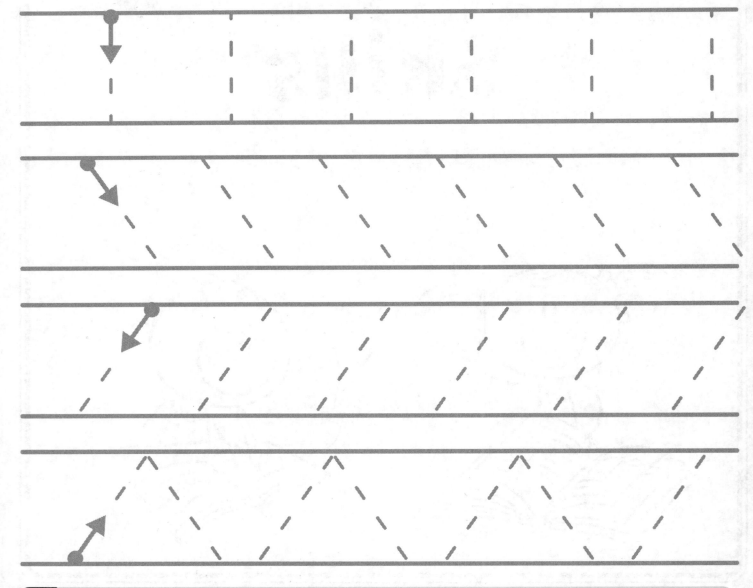

Trace the lines below.
Circle your best traced line.

## Think About it!

Why don't crabs like to share?
Because they're a little shellfish!

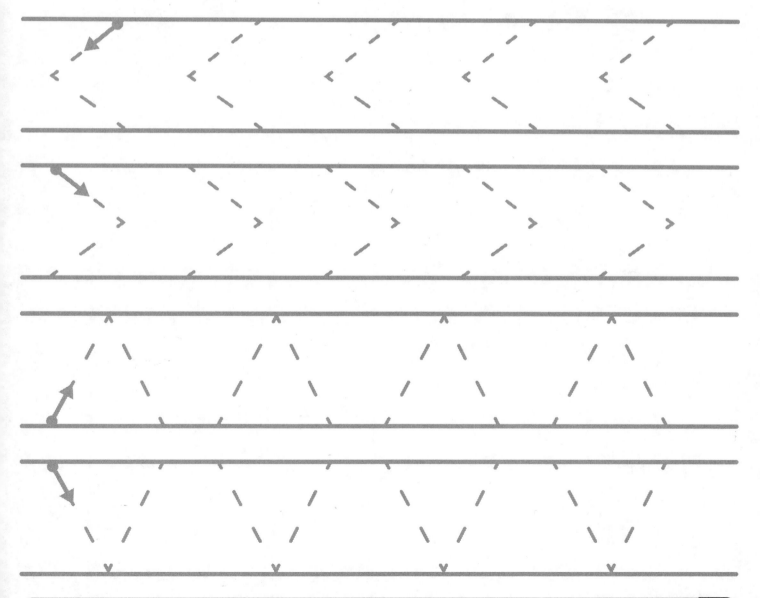

Trace the lines below.
Circle your best traced line.

## Think About it!

What's a dog's favourite kind of pizza?
Pupperoni pizza!

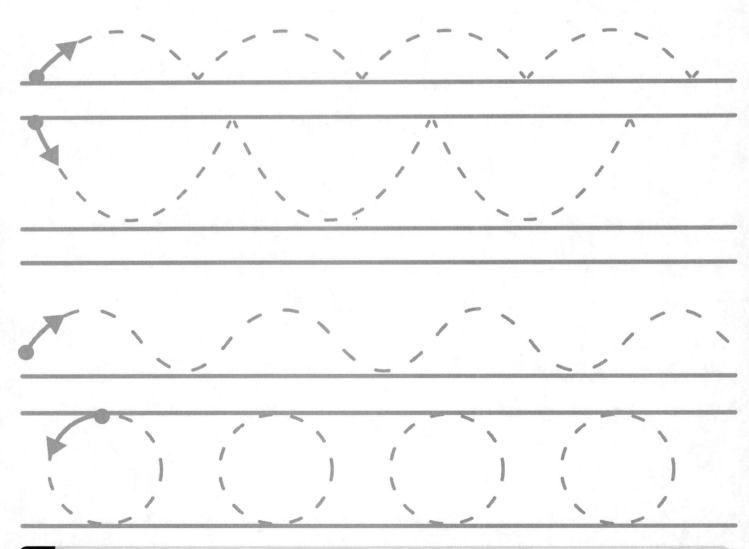

Trace the lines below.
Circle your best traced line.

## Think About it!

What does a turtle do on it's birthday?
It shellebrates!

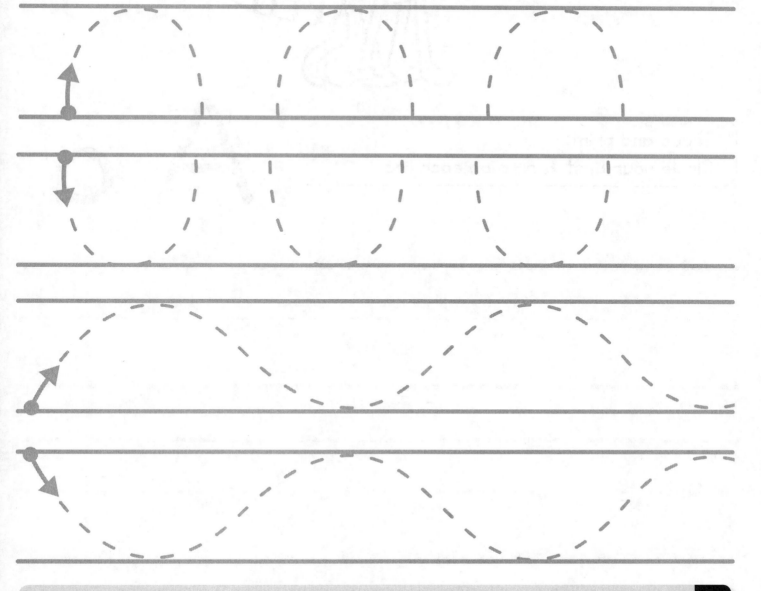

# A is for ant.

Trace and print.
Circle your best A or a on each line.

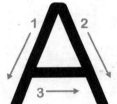 

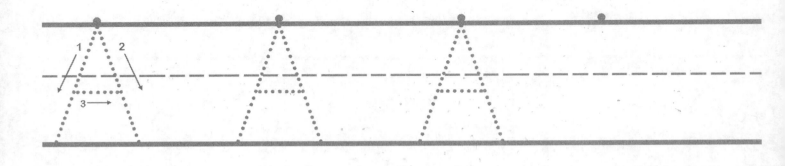

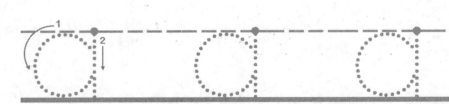

Colour the apples with a capital A green.
Colour the apples with a lowercase a red.

Trace and print.
Circle your best A or a on each line.

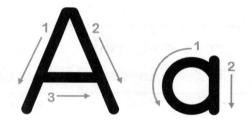

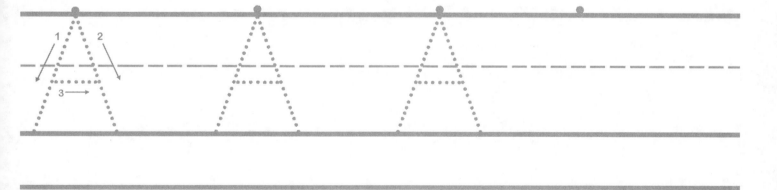

# B is for bee.

Trace and print.
Circle your best B or b on each line.

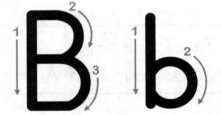

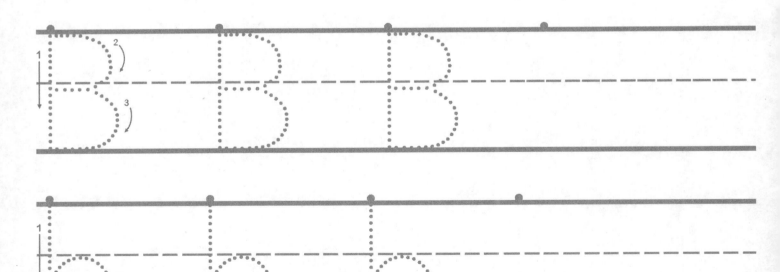

Colour the books with a capital B yellow.
Colour the books with a lowercase b blue.

Trace and print.
Circle your best B or b on each line.

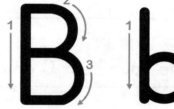

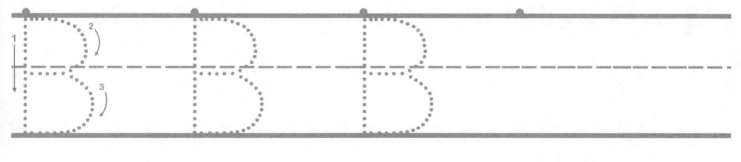

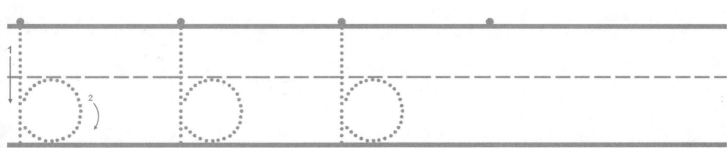

# C is for cow.

Trace and print.
Circle your best C or c on each line.

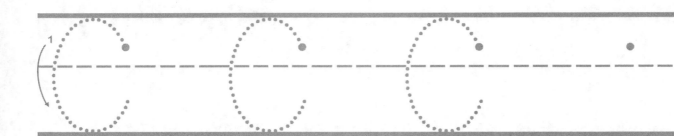

Colour the circles with a capital C purple.
Colour the circles with a lowercase c red.

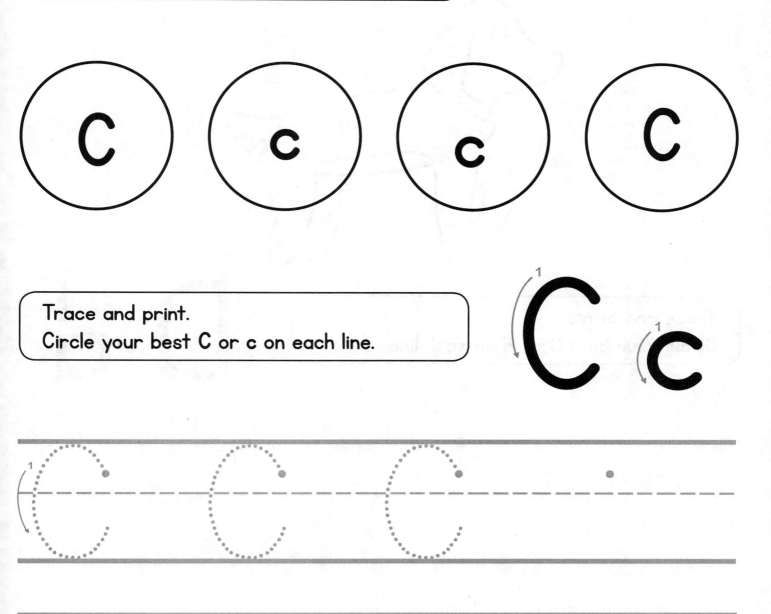

Trace and print.
Circle your best C or c on each line.

# D is for dog.

Trace and print.
Circle your best D or d on each line.

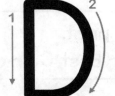

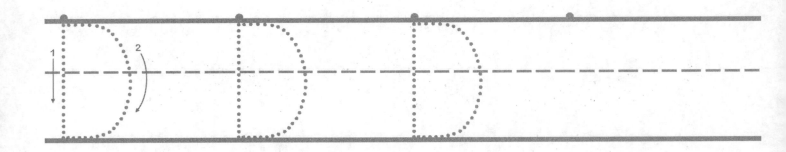

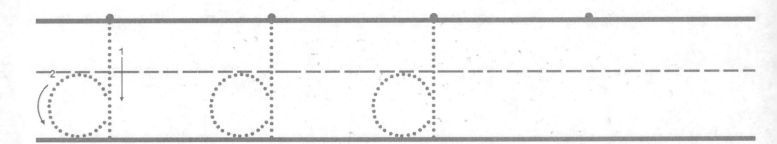

Colour the drums with a capital D purple.
Colour the drums with a lowercase d brown.

Trace and print.
Circle your best D or d on each line.

# E is for eagle.

Trace and print.
Circle your best E or e on each line.

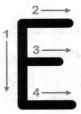 

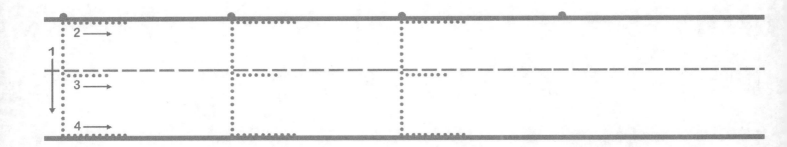

Colour the eggs with a capital E yellow.
Colour the eggs with a lowercase e green.

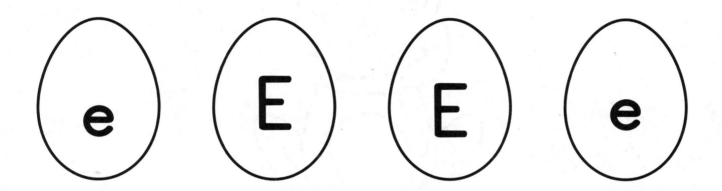

Trace and print.
Circle your best E or e on each line.

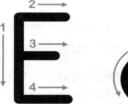 

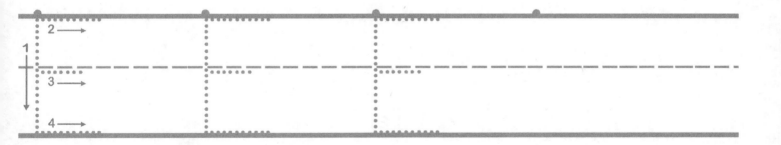

# F is for frog.

Trace and print.
Circle your best F or f on each line.

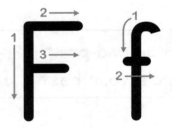

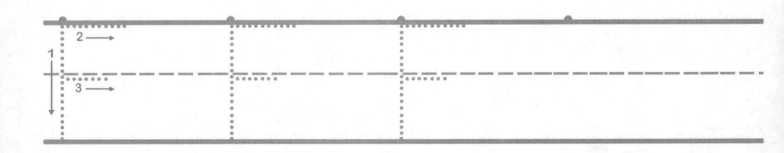

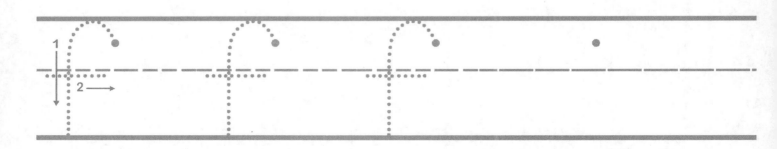

Colour the fish with a capital F orange.
Colour the fish with a lowercase f blue.

Trace and print.
Circle your best F or f on each line.

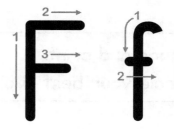

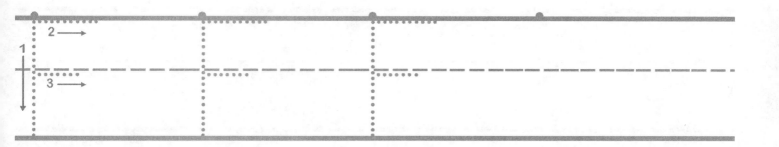

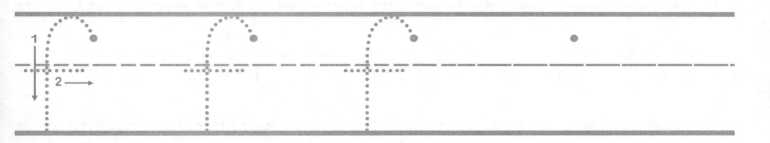

# G is for goat.

Trace and print.
Circle your best G or g on each line.

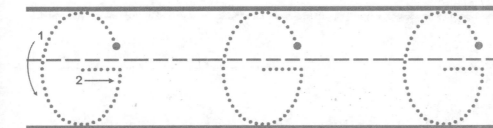

Colour the gloves with a capital G orange.
Colour the gloves with a lowercase g blue.

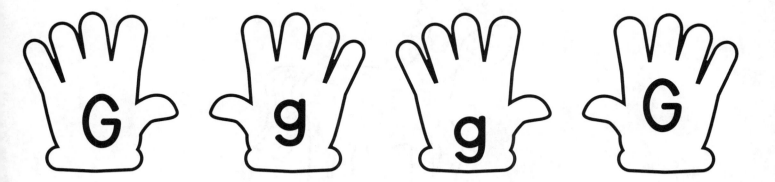

Trace and print.
Circle your best G or g on each line.

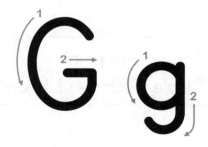

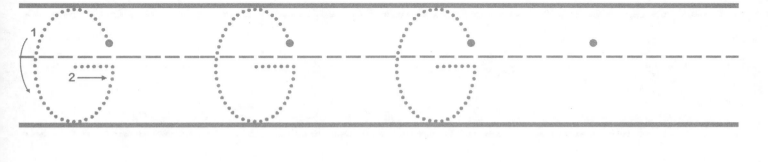

# H is for horse.

Trace and print.
Circle your best H or h on each line.

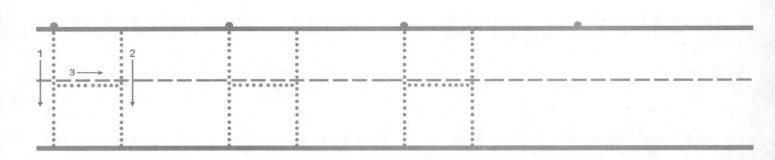

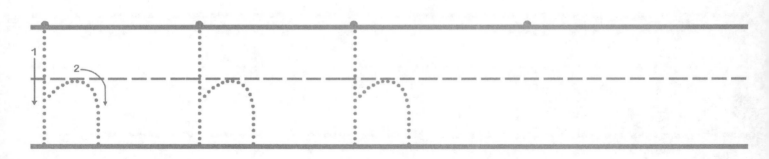

# Letter Hh

Colour the houses with a capital H orange.
Colour the houses with a lowercase h blue.

Trace and print.
Circle your best H or h on each line.

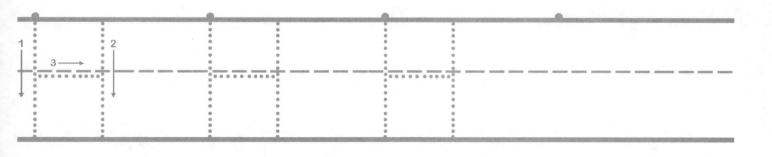

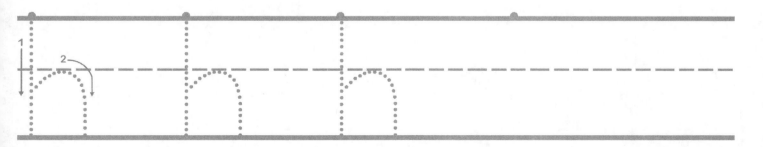

# I is for iguana.

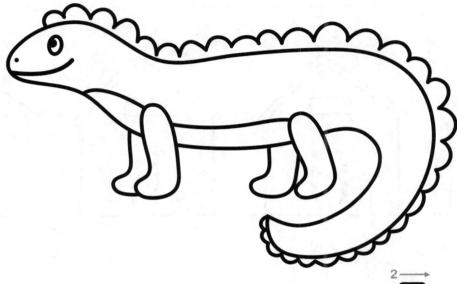

Trace and print.
Circle your best I or i on each line.

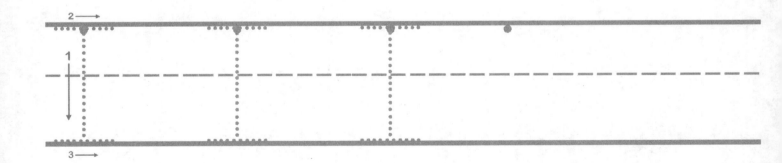

# Letter Ii

Colour the igloos with a capital I orange.
Colour the igloos with a lowercase i blue.

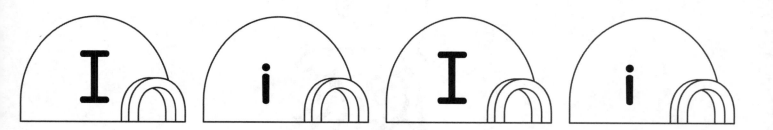

Trace and print.
Circle your best I or i on each line.

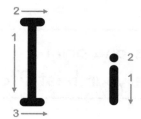

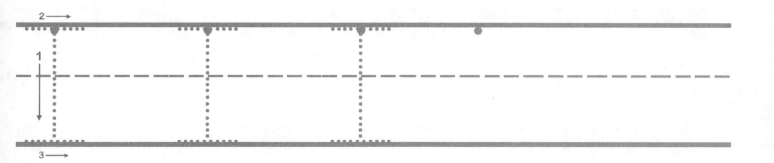

# J is for jellyfish.

Trace and print.
Circle your best **J** or **j** on each line.

# Letter Jj

Colour the jugs with a capital J orange.
Colour the jugs with a lowercase j blue.

Trace and print.
Circle your best J or j on each line.

# K is for kangaroo.

Trace and print.
Circle your best K or k on each line.

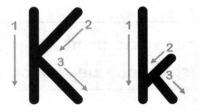

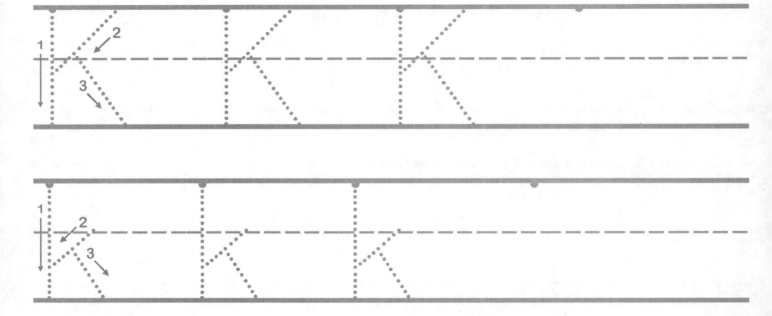

Colour the kites with a capital K orange.
Colour the kites with a lowercase k blue.

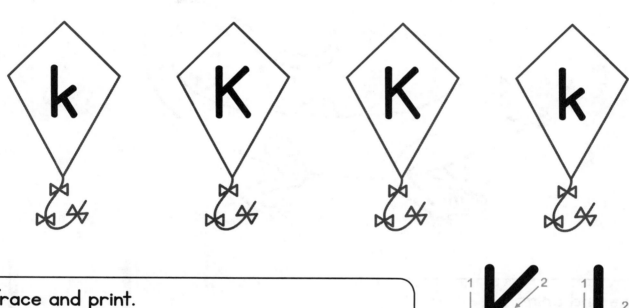

Trace and print.
Circle your best K or k on each line.

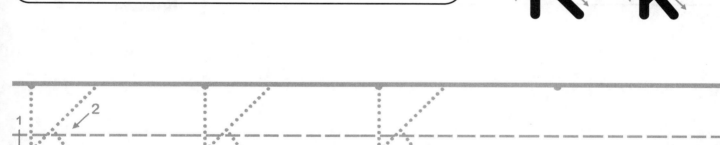

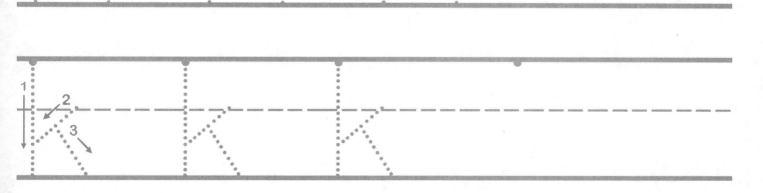

# L is for lizard.

Trace and print.
Circle your best L or l on each line.

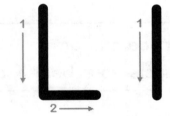

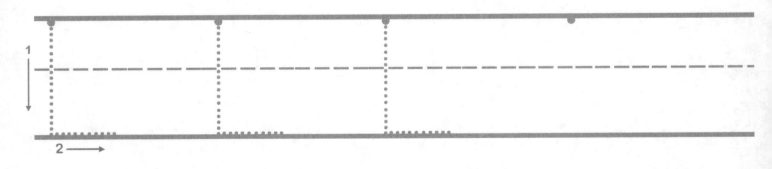

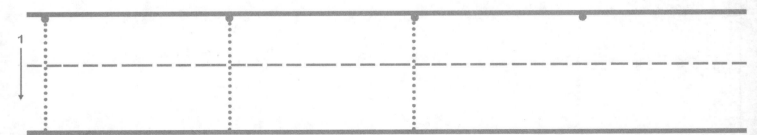

Colour the lemons with a capital L yellow.
Colour the lemons with a lowercase l blue.

Trace and print.
Circle your best L or l on each line.

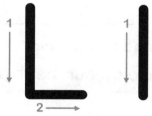

# M is for mouse.

Trace and print.
Circle your best M or m on each line.

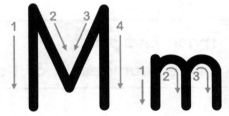

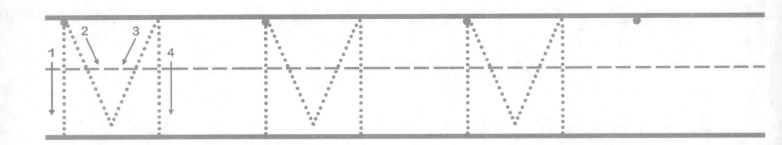

Colour the mushrooms with a capital M orange.
Colour the mushrooms with a lowercase m blue.

Trace and print.
Circle your best M or m on each line.

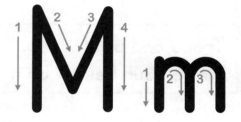

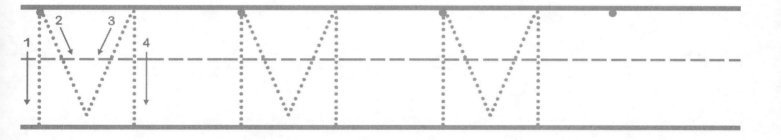

# N is for narwhal.

Trace and print.
Circle your best N or n on each line.

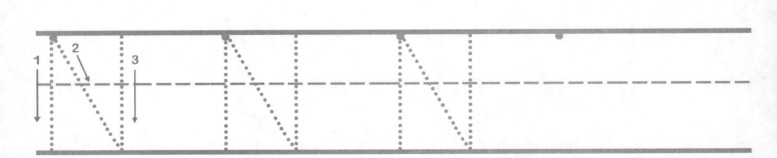

Colour the neckties with a capital N orange.
Colour the neckties with a lowercase n blue.

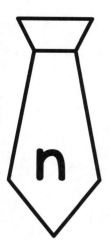   

Trace and print.
Circle your best N or n on each line.

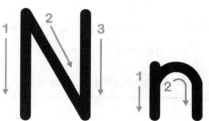

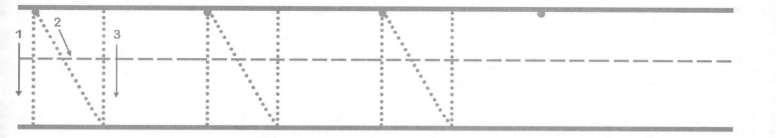

# O is for ostrich.

Trace and print.
Circle your best O or o on each line.

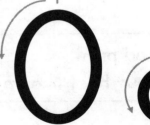

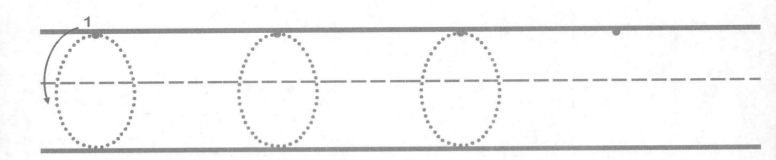

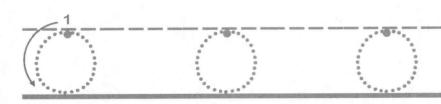

Colour the oranges with a capital O orange.
Colour the oranges with a lowercase o blue.

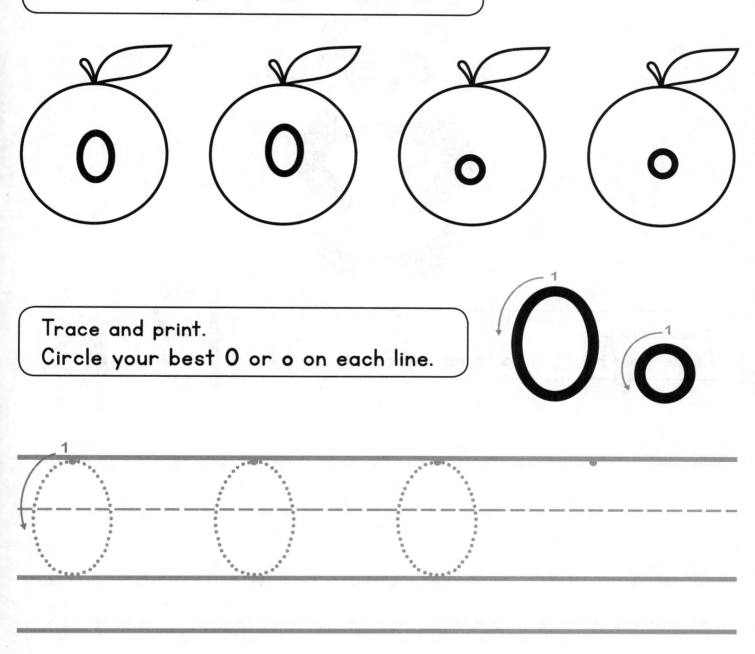

Trace and print.
Circle your best O or o on each line.

# P is for panda.

Trace and print.
Circle your best P or p on each line.

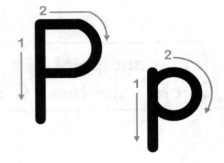

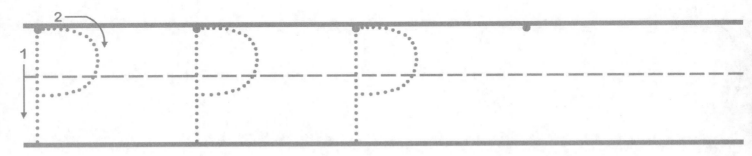

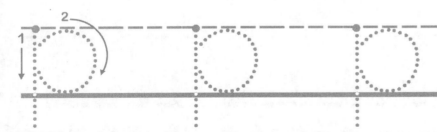

Colour the puzzle pieces with a capital P red.
Colour the puzzle pieces with a lowercase p blue.

Trace and print.
Circle your best P or p on each line.

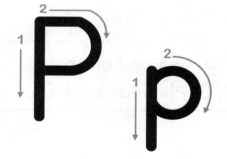

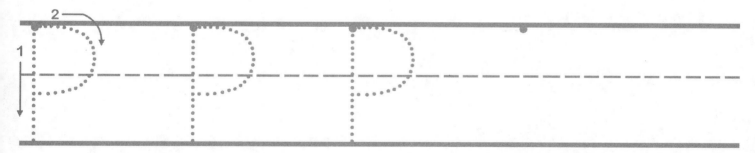

# Q is for quail.

Trace and print.
Circle your best Q or q on each line.

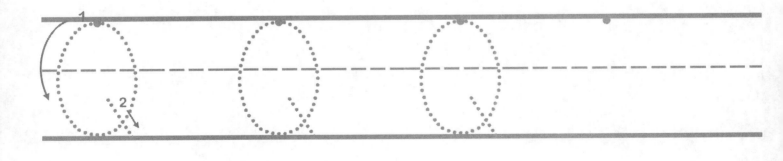

Colour the quils with a capital Q purple.
Colour the quils with a lowercase q green.

Trace and print.
Circle your best Q or q on each line.

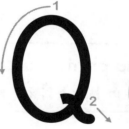 

# R is for raccoon.

Trace and print.
Circle your best R or r on each line.

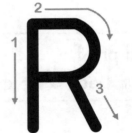

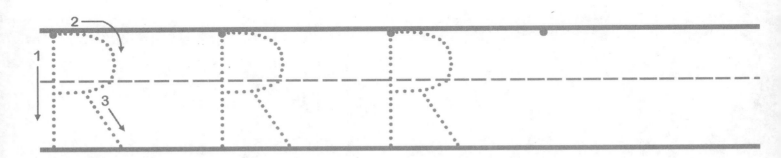

Colour the rain clouds with a capital R yellow.
Colour the rain clouds with a lowercase r red.

Trace and print.
Circle your best R or r on each line.

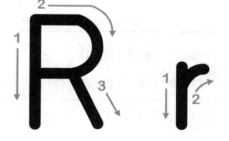

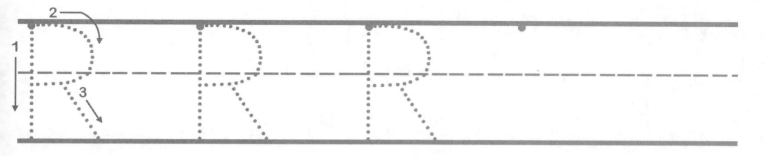

# S is for seagull.

Trace and print.
Circle your best S or s on each line.

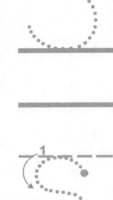

Colour the stars with a capital S orange.
Colour the stars with a lowercase s green.

Trace and print.
Circle your best S or s on each line.

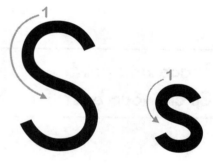

# T is for turtle.

Trace and print.
Circle your best T or t on each line.

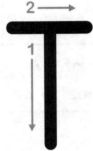

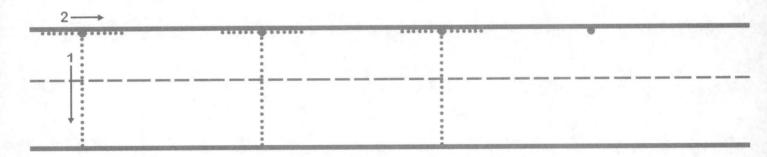

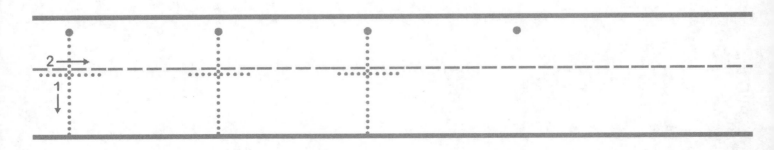

Colour the triangles with a capital T orange.
Colour the triangles with a lowercase t purple.

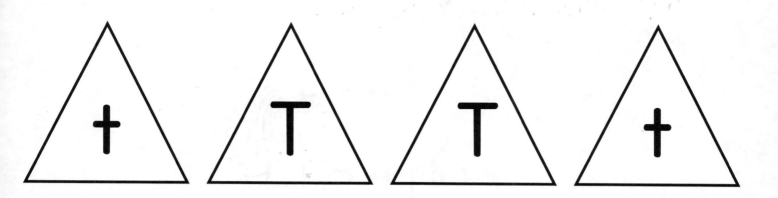

Trace and print.
Circle your best T or t on each line.

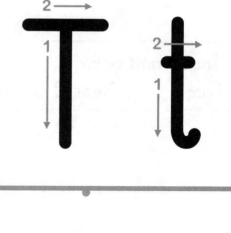

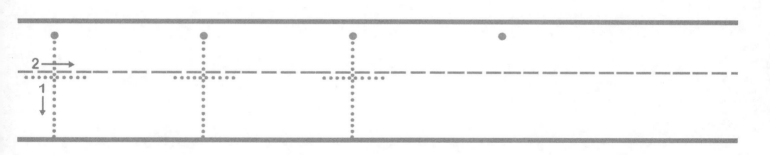

# U is for unicorn.

Trace and print.
Circle your best U or u on each line.

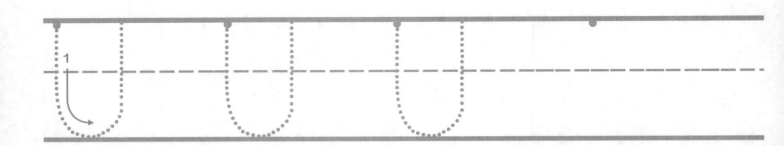

Colour the umbrellas with a capital U yelow.
Colour the umbrellas with a lowercase u blue.

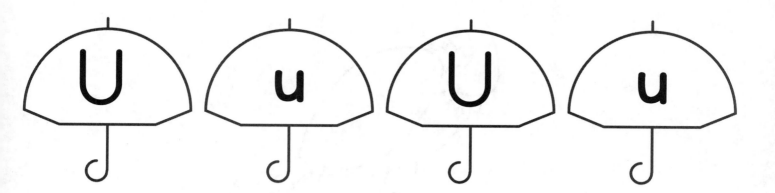

Trace and print.
Circle your best U or u on each line.

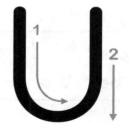

# V is for vulture.

Trace and print.
Circle your best V or v on each line.

Colour the vases with a capital V green.
Colour the vases with a lowercase v orange.

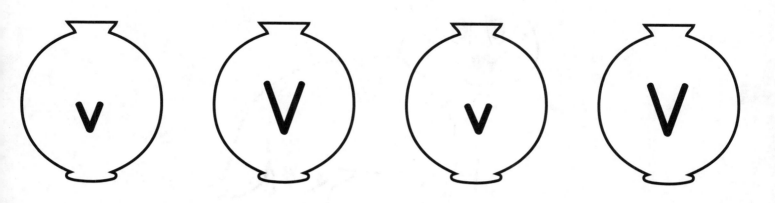

Trace and print.
Circle your best V or v on each line.

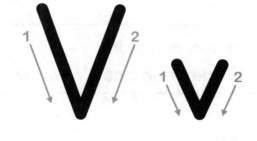

# W is for wolf.

Trace and print.
Circle your best W or w on each line.

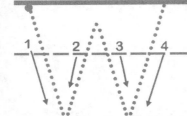

Colour the wedges with a capital W purple.
Colour the wedges with a lowercase w red.

Trace and print.
Circle your best W or w on each line.

# X is for x-ray fish.

Trace and print.
Circle your best X or x on each line.

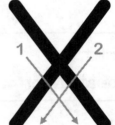

Colour the xylophones with a capital X blue.
Colour the xylophones with a lowercase x green.

Trace and print.
Circle your best X or x on each line.

# Y is for yak.

Trace and print.
Circle your best Y or y on each line.

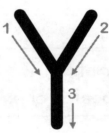
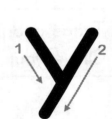

# Letter Yy

Colour the yo-yos with a capital Y orange.
Colour the yo-yos with a lowercase y blue.

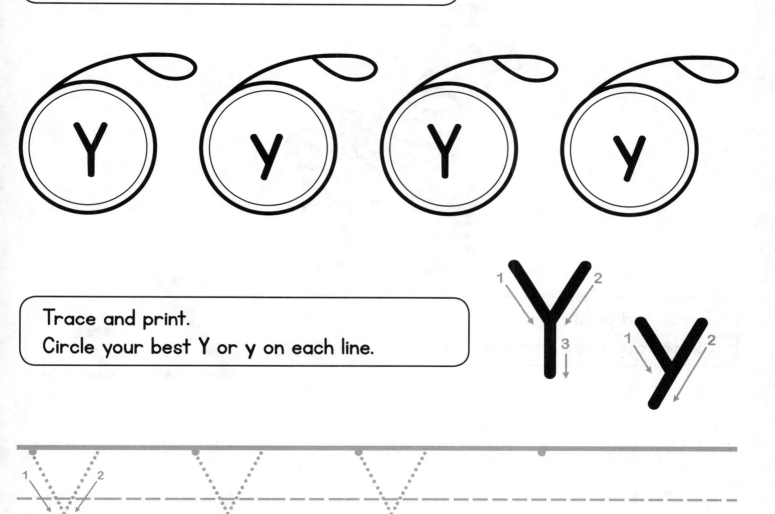

Trace and print.
Circle your best Y or y on each line.

# Z is for zebra.

Trace and print.
Circle your best Z or z on each line.

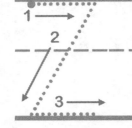

Colour the zig-zags with a capital **Z** green.
Colour the zig-zags with a lowercase **z** yellow.

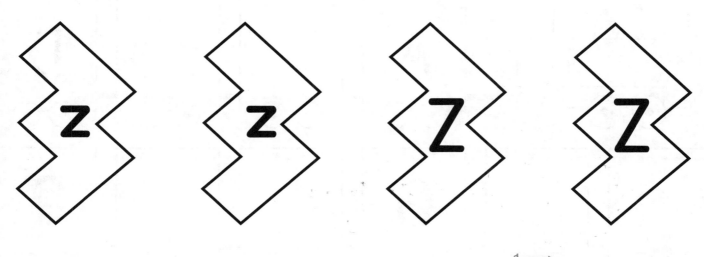

Trace and print.
Circle your best **Z** or **z** on each line.

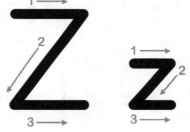

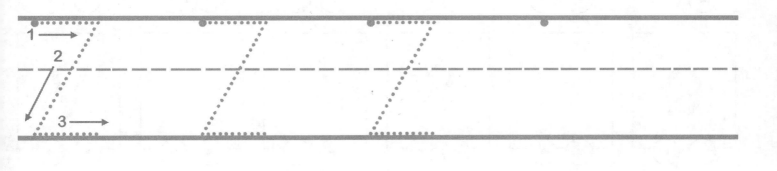

# Alphabet Train Fun

Fill in the missing uppercase letters of the alphabet.
Colour the train.

# Reading Readiness

# Beginning Letter Sounds

Say the name of the picture out loud. Print the beginning letter sound.

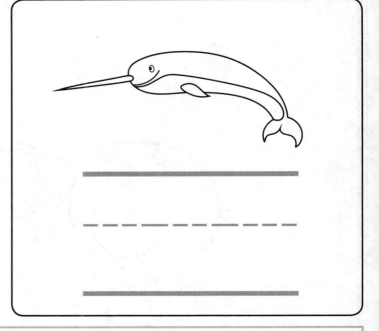

Colour the zebra. red    Colour the frog. green

Colour the unicorn. purple    Colour the narwhal. blue

Say the name of the picture out loud. Print the beginning letter sound.

Colour the kangaroo. [ purple ]    Colour the dog. [ orange ]

Colour the seagull. [ yellow ]    Colour the lizard. [ green ]

# Beginning Letter Sounds

Say the name of the picture out loud. Print the beginning letter sound.

Colour the wolf.　blue

Colour the panda.　red

Colour the quail.　green

Colour the bee.　yellow

# Beginning Letter Sounds

Say the name of the picture out loud. Print the beginning letter sound.

_____

- - - - - - - - - - - -

_____

_____

- - - - - - - - - - - -

_____

_____

- - - - - - - - - - - -

_____

_____

- - - - - - - - - - - -

_____

Colour the eagle. ⬤ orange ▷

Colour the ostrich. ⬤ purple ▷

Colour the turtle. ⬤ green ▷

Colour the iguana. ⬤ blue ▷

# Beginning Letter Sounds

Say the name of the picture out loud. Print the beginning letter sound.

_____

- - - - - - - - - - - - - -

_____

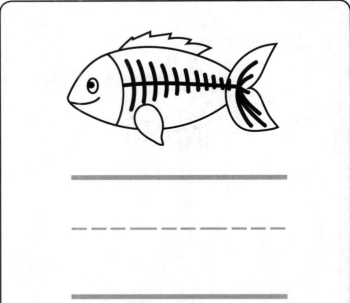

_____

- - - - - - - - - - - - - -

_____

_____

- - - - - - - - - - - - - -

_____

_____

- - - - - - - - - - - - - -

_____

Colour the goat. ( red )     Colour the x-ray fish. ( green )

Colour the ant. ( yellow )     Colour the horse. ( blue )

# Beginning Letter Sounds

Say the name of the picture out loud. Print the beginning letter sound.

Colour the cow. 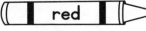 red

Colour the jellyfish. blue

Colour the yak. green

Colour the vulture. black

# Beginning Letter Sounds

Say the name of the picture out loud. Print the beginning letter sound.

_____

- - - - - - - - - - - -

_____

_____

- - - - - - - - - - - -

_____

Colour the mouse. ([ red ]➤   Colour the raccoon. ([ green ]➤

## Draw a picture of your favourite animal.

Print the beginning letter sound of the animal.

- - - - - - - - - -

_____

# Beginning Letter Sounds

Colour the pictures that have the beginning sound of the letter in the box.

# Beginning Letter Sounds

Colour the pictures that have the beginning sound of the letter in the box.

# Beginning Letter Sounds

Colour the pictures that have the beginning sound of the letter in the box.

# Beginning Letter Sounds

Colour the pictures that have the beginning sound of the letter in the box.

# Beginning Letter Sounds

Colour the pictures that have the beginning sound of the letter in the box.

# Beginning Letter Sounds

Colour the pictures that have the beginning sound of the letter in the box.

# Beginning Letter Sounds

Colour the pictures that have the beginning sound of the letter in the box.

# Beginning Letter Sounds

Colour the pictures that have the beginning sound of the letter in the box.

# Beginning Letter Sounds

Colour the pictures that have the beginning sound of the letter in the box.

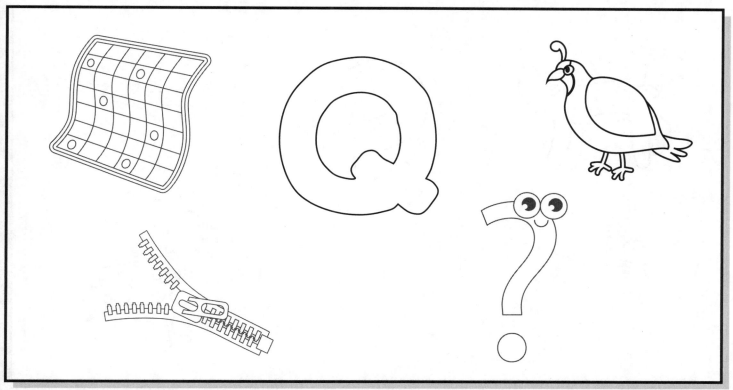

# Beginning Letter Sounds

Colour the pictures that have the beginning sound of the letter in the box.

# Beginning Letter Sounds

Colour the pictures that have the beginning sound of the letter in the box.

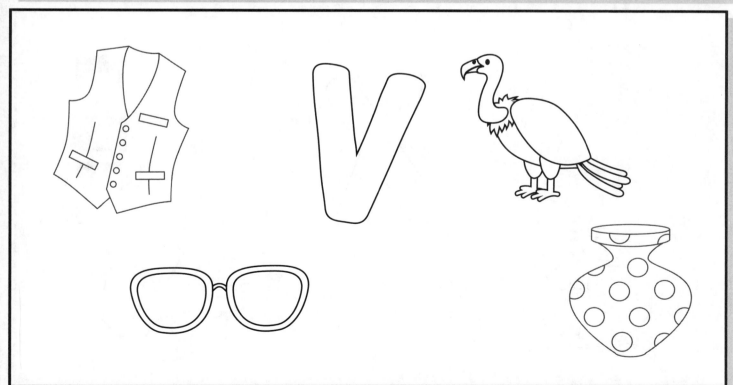

# Beginning Letter Sounds

Colour the pictures that have the beginning sound of the letter in the box.

# Beginning Letter Sounds

Colour the pictures that have the beginning sound of the letter in the box.

# Beginning Letter Sound Match

Say the name of each picture out loud. Draw a line from the picture to the correct beginning letter sound. Colour the pictures.

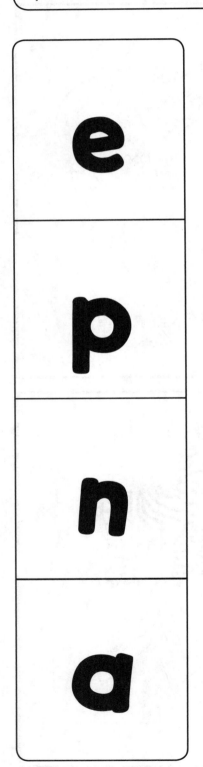

# Beginning Letter Sound Match

Say the name of each picture out loud. Draw a line from the picture to the correct beginning letter sound. Colour the pictures.

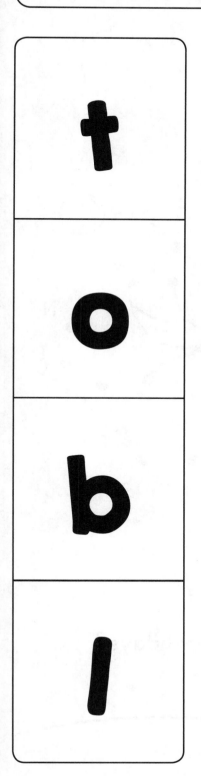

## Think About it!

What do turtles do on their birthdays?
They shellebrate!

# Number and Counting Skills

# Number 0

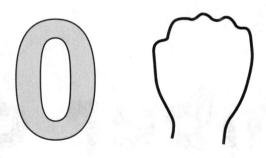

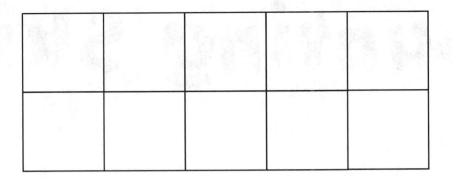

Trace and print.
Circle your best 0 on each line.

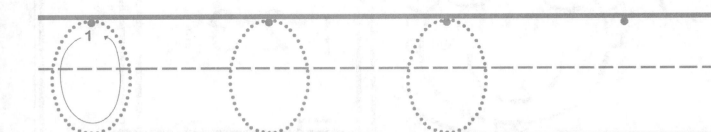

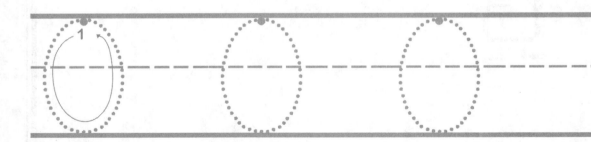

Count the gum balls in the machine.
Circle the correct number.

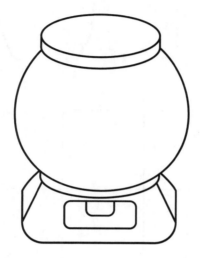

0   1   2

Draw 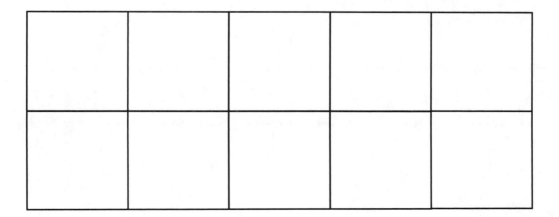 to show the number 0.

| | | | | |
|---|---|---|---|---|
| | | | | |

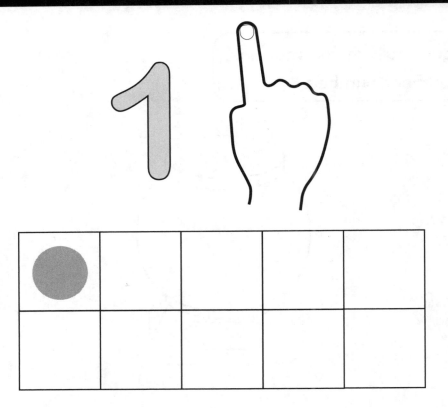

Trace and print.
Circle your best 1 on each line.

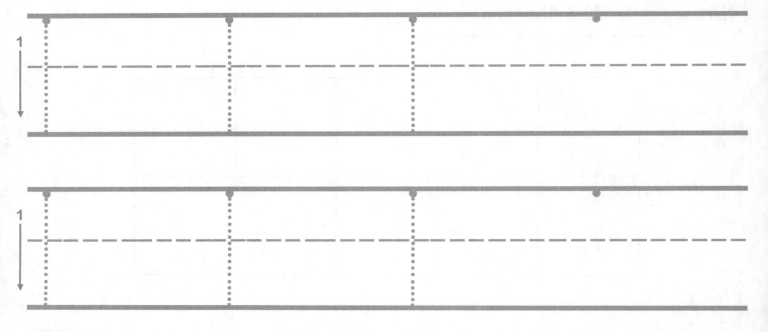

# Number 1

Count the narwhal.
Circle the correct number.

0    1    2

Draw ⬤ to show the number 1.

| | | | | |
|---|---|---|---|---|
| | | | | |

Trace and print.
Circle your best 2 on each line.

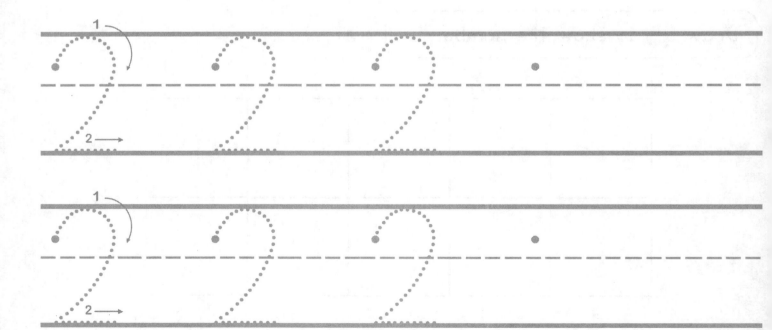

Count the frogs.
Circle the correct number.

0   1   2

Draw ● to show the number 2.

# Number 3

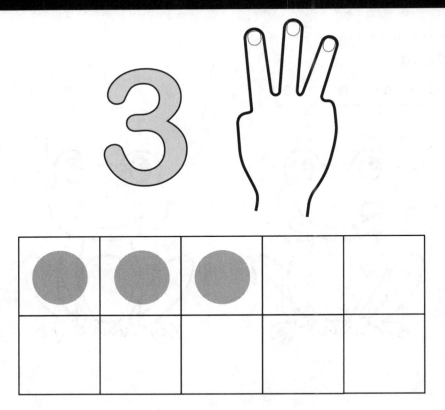

Trace and print.
Circle your best 3 on each line.

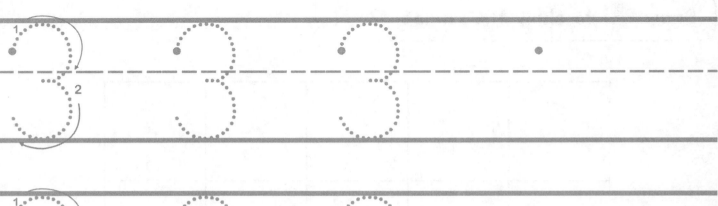

Count the lizards.
Circle the correct number.

## 3   4   5

Draw ● to show the number 3.

| | | | | |
|---|---|---|---|---|
| | | | | |
| | | | | |

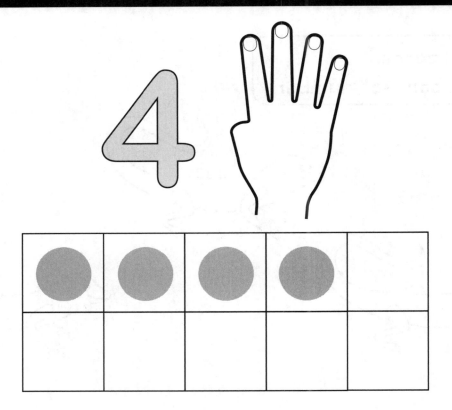

Trace and print.
Circle your best 4 on each line.

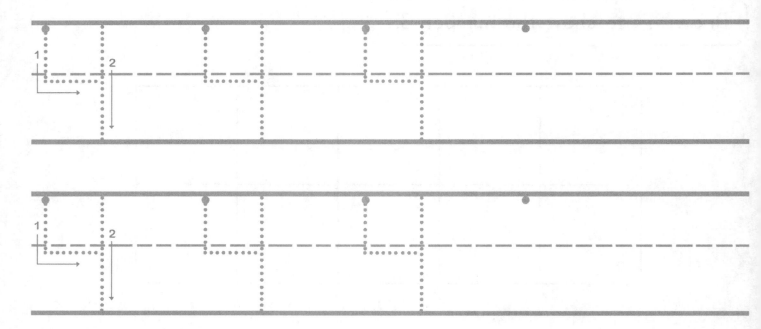

Count the dogs.
Circle the correct number.

# 3  4  5

Draw ⬤ to show the number 4.

|  |  |  |  |  |
|--|--|--|--|--|
|  |  |  |  |  |

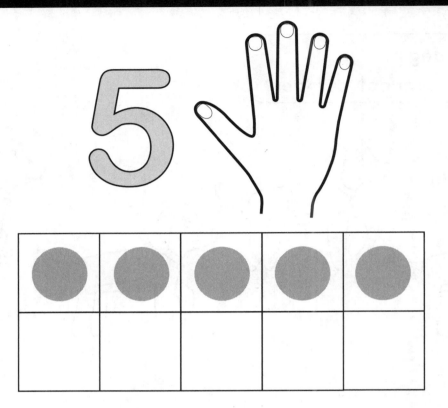

Trace and print.
Circle your best **5** on each line.

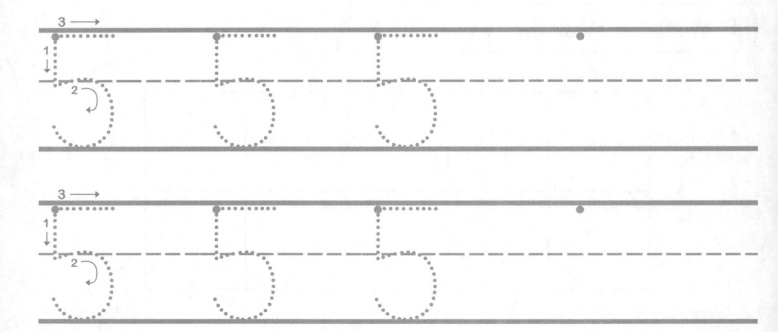

Count the seagulls.
Circle the correct number.

# 3  4  5

Draw ⬤ to show the number 5.

|  |  |  |  |  |
|--|--|--|--|--|
|  |  |  |  |  |
|  |  |  |  |  |

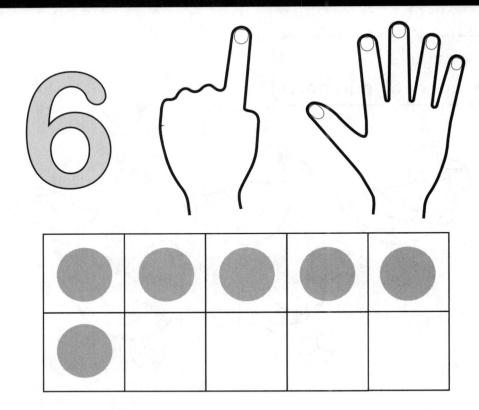

Trace and print.
Circle your best 6 on each line.

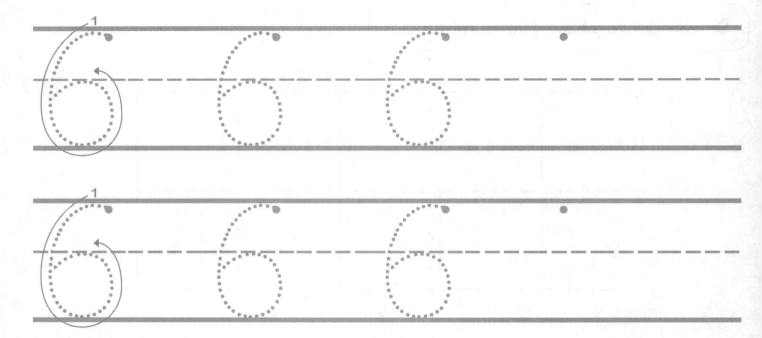

# Number 6

Count the kangaroos.
Circle the correct number.

# 6  7  8

Draw ● to show the number 6.

| | | | | |
|---|---|---|---|---|
| | | | | |

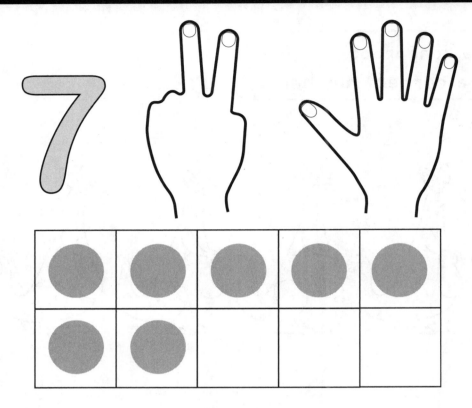

Trace and print.
Circle your best 7 on each line.

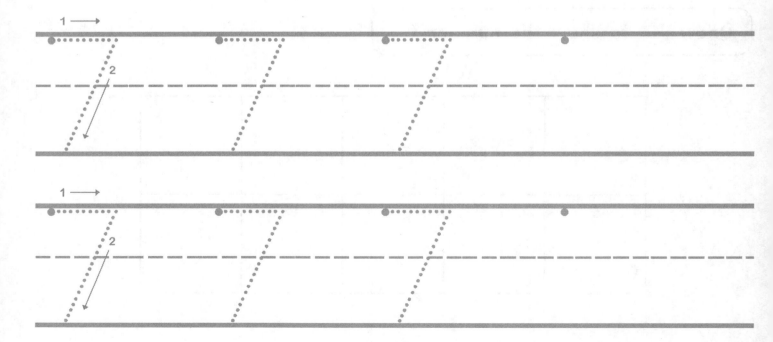

Count the eagles.
Circle the correct number.

6    7    8

Draw ● to show the number 7.

|  |  |  |  |  |
|---|---|---|---|---|
|  |  |  |  |  |
|  |  |  |  |  |

# Number 8

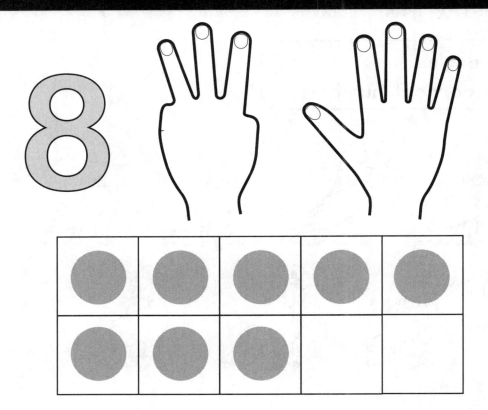

Trace and print.
Circle your best **8** on each line.

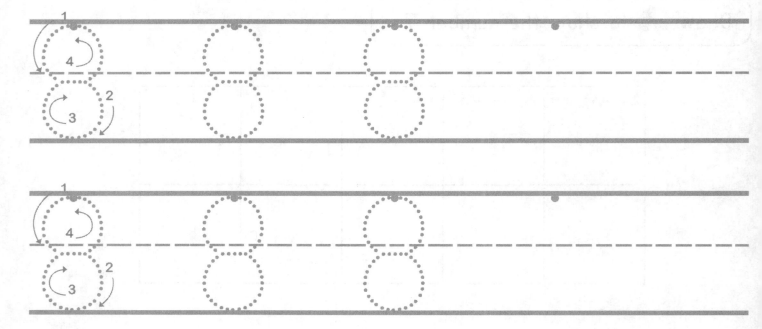

Count the panda bears.
Circle the correct number.

6    7    8

Draw ● to show the number 8.

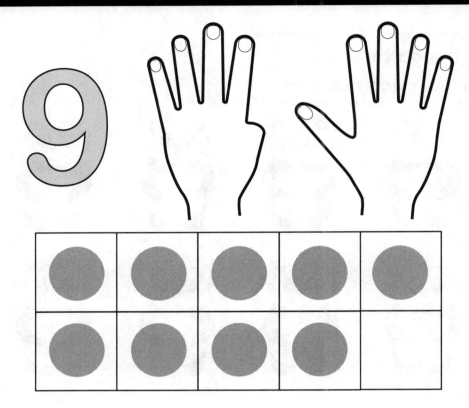

Trace and print.
Circle your best 9 on each line.

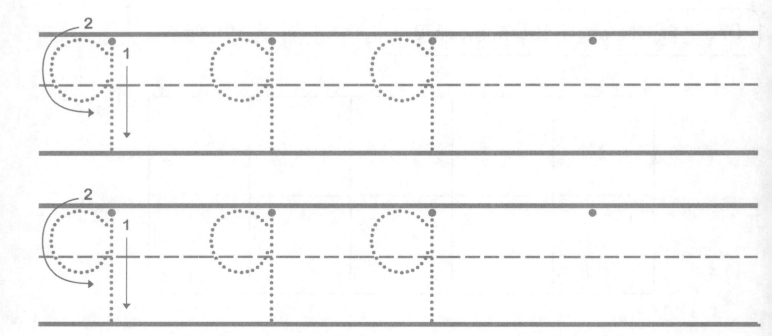

Count the jellyfish.
Circle the correct number.

## 8   9   10

Draw ● to show the number 9.

| | | | | |
|---|---|---|---|---|
| | | | | |

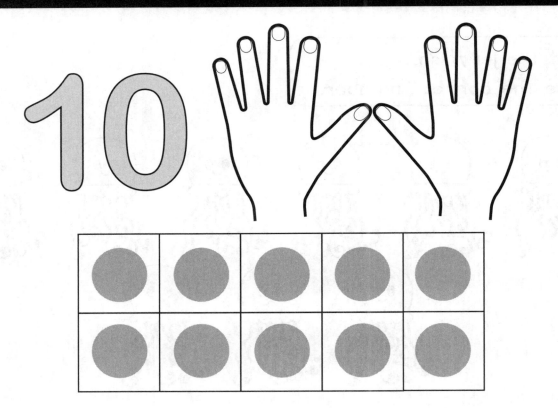

Trace and print.
Circle your best 10 on each line.

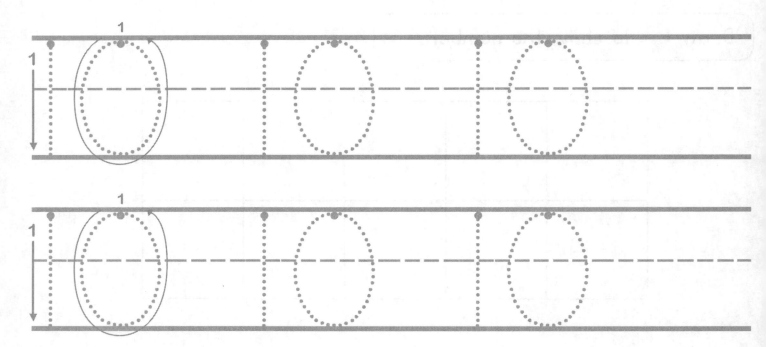

Count the mice.
Circle the correct number.

8    9    10

Draw ● to show the number 10.

# Counting Practice

How many fingers are there? Use your fingers to count. Circle the correct number.

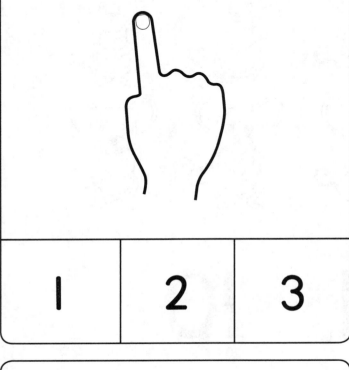

| 1 | 2 | 3 |

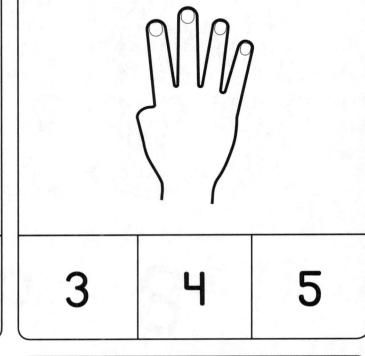

| 3 | 4 | 5 |

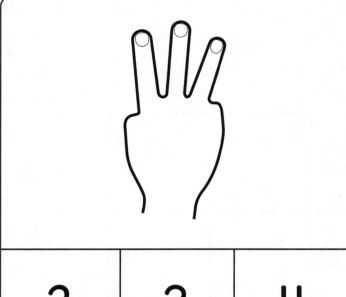

| 2 | 3 | 4 |

| 7 | 8 | 9 |

# Counting Practice

How many fingers are there? Use your fingers to count. Circle the correct number.

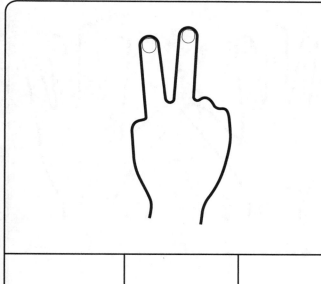

| 1 | 2 | 3 |
|---|---|---|

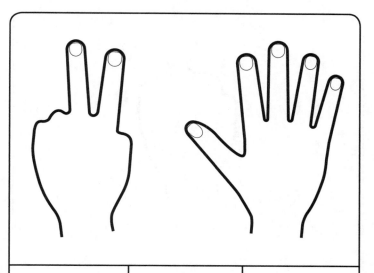

| 6 | 7 | 8 |
|---|---|---|

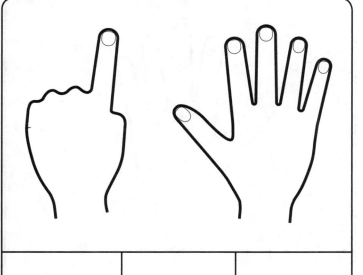

| 6 | 7 | 8 |
|---|---|---|

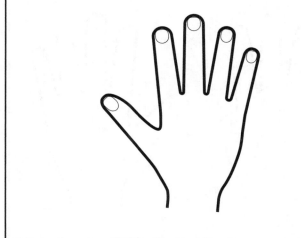

| 3 | 4 | 5 |
|---|---|---|

# Counting Practice

How many fingers are there? Use your fingers to count. Circle the correct number.

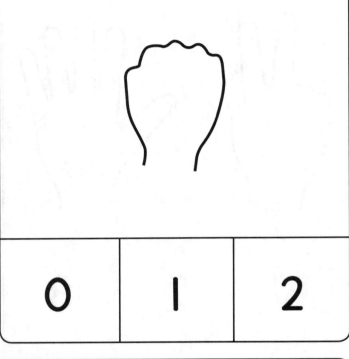

| 0 | 1 | 2 |
|---|---|---|

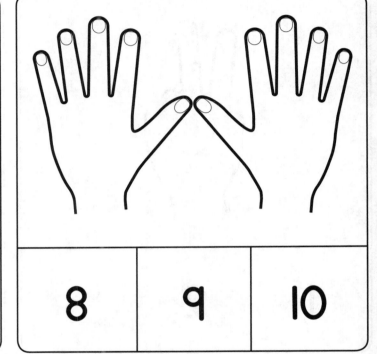

| 8 | 9 | 10 |
|---|---|---|

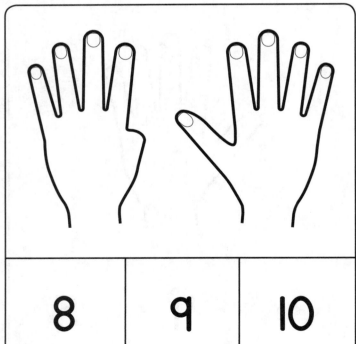

| 8 | 9 | 10 |
|---|---|---|

| 4 | 5 | 6 |
|---|---|---|

# Counting Practice

How many shapes are there? Count the shapes and print the number below. Colour the shapes.

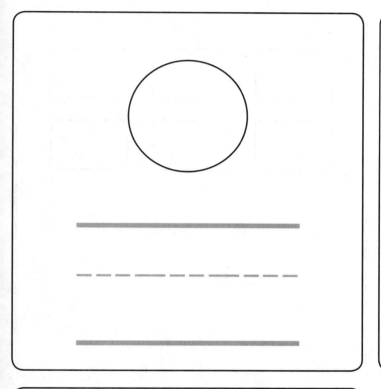

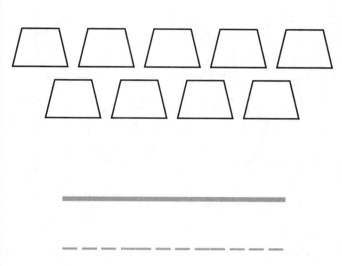

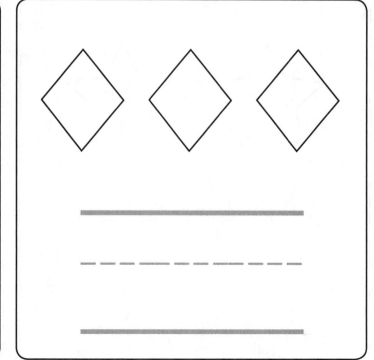

# Counting Practice

How many shapes are there? Count the shapes and print the number below. Colour the shapes.

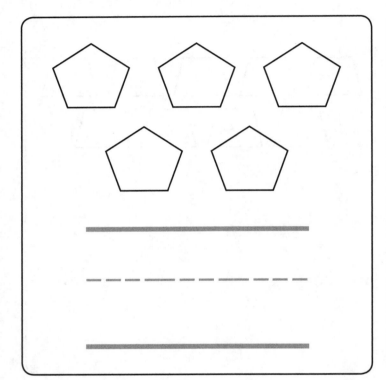

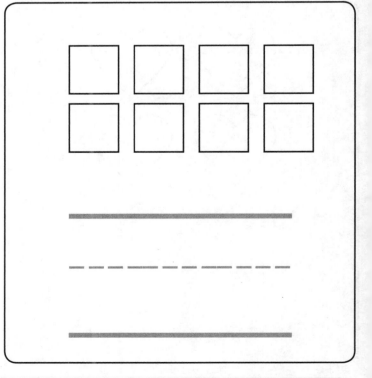

# Counting Practice

How many shapes are there? Count the shapes and print the number below. Colour the shapes.

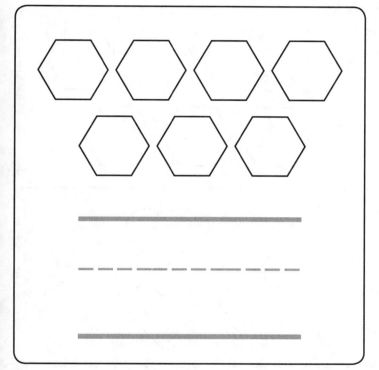

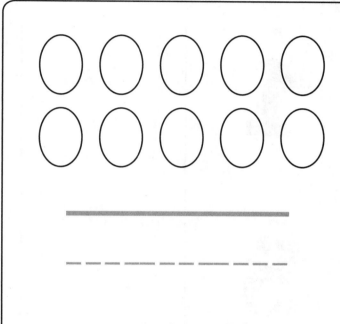

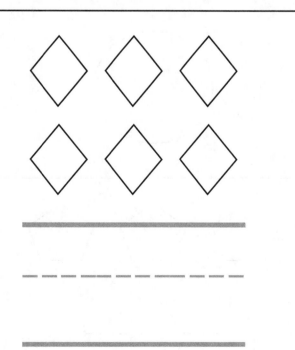

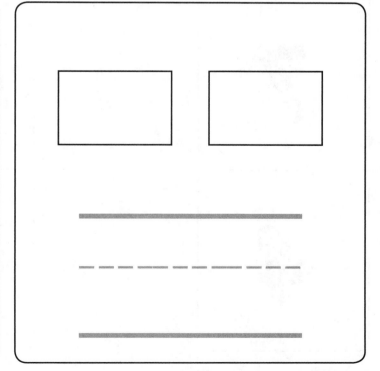

Read the numbers. Count the shapes. Draw a line from the number to the correct shapes. Colour the shapes.

**1**

**5**

**7**

**4**

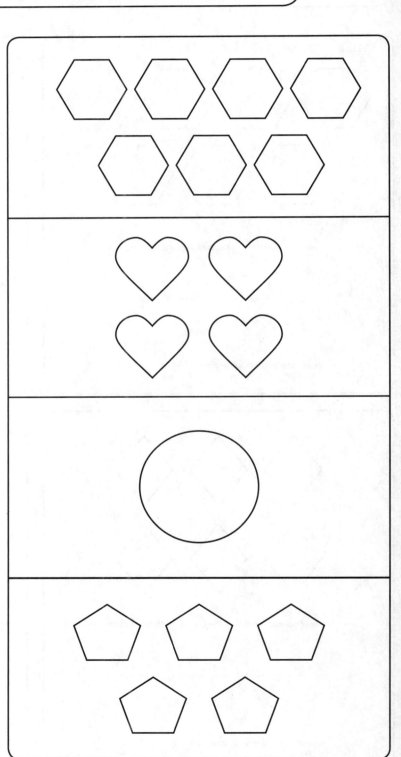

Read the numbers. Count the shapes. Draw a line from the number to the correct shapes. Colour the shapes.

| 2 |
| 8 |
| 9 |
| 3 |

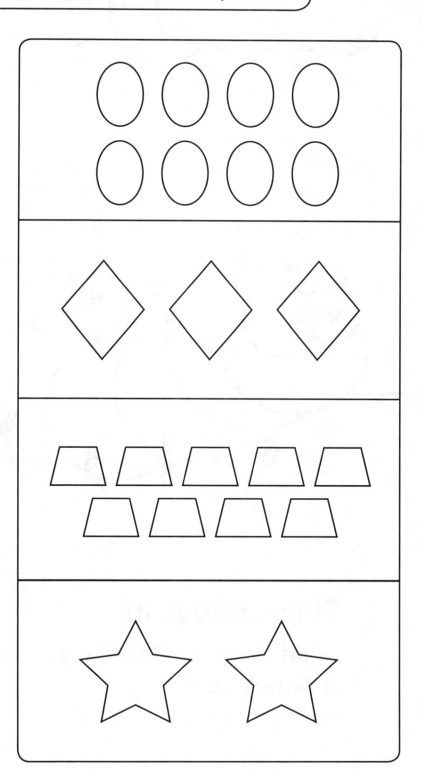

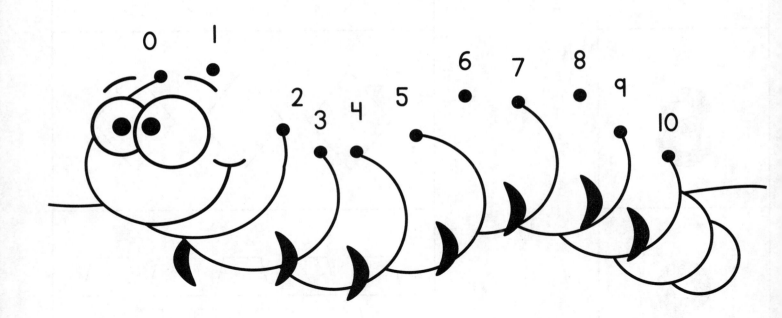

## Think About it!

What does a butterfly go to sleep on?
A Caterpillow!

## Think About it!

What's the most expensive fish?
A Goldfish!

# Colouring By Number

Use the colour key to colour in the picture.

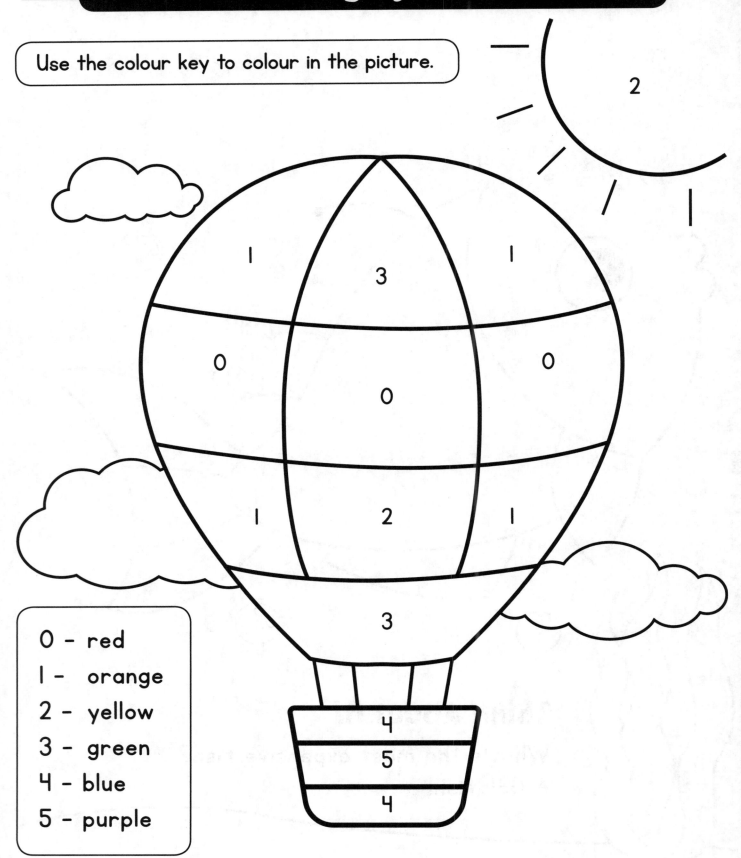

0 - red
1 - orange
2 - yellow
3 - green
4 - blue
5 - purple

# Colouring By Number

Use the colour key to colour in the picture.

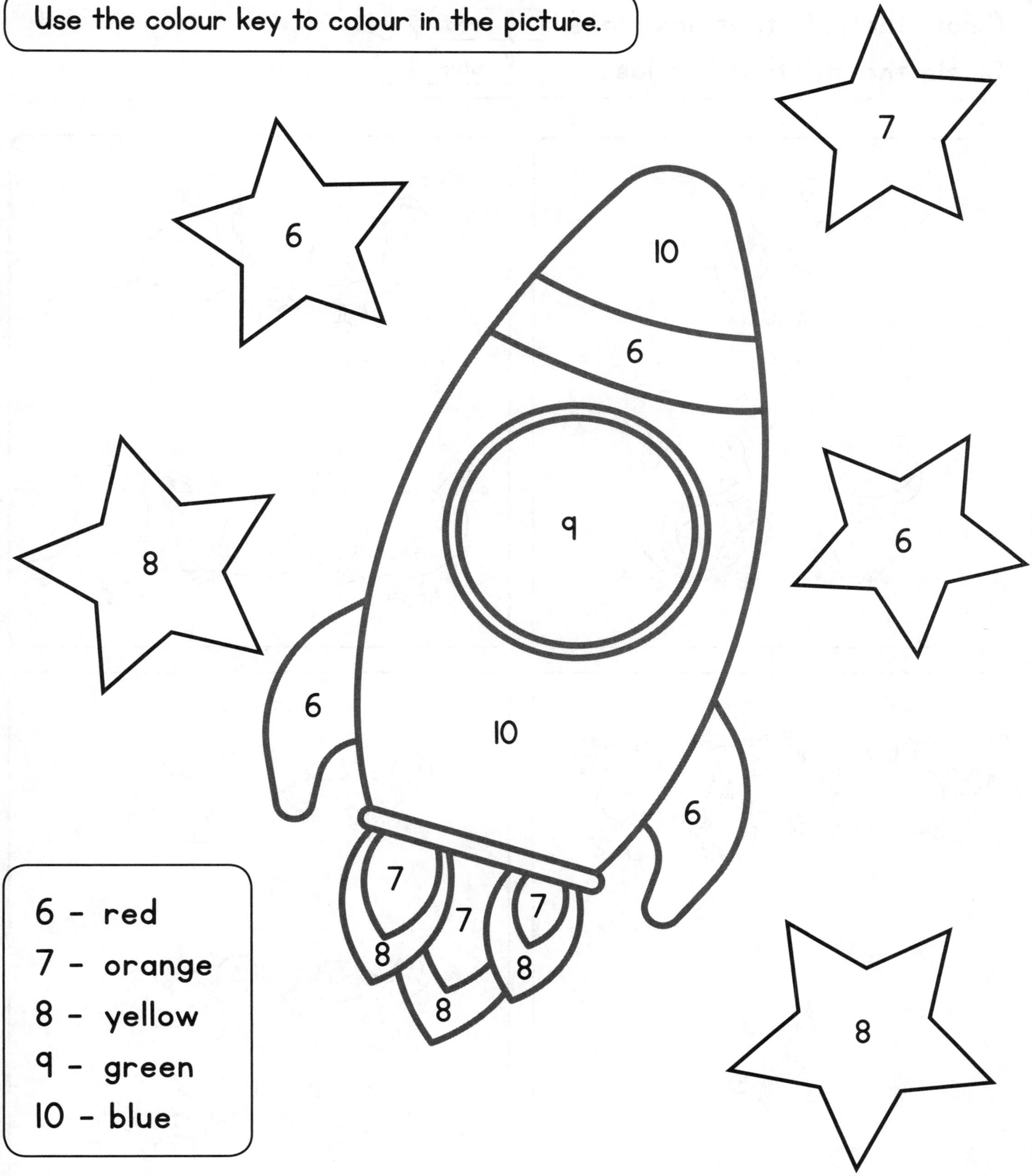

6 - red
7 - orange
8 - yellow
9 - green
10 - blue

# Comparing Sets

Circle the set  that has **more**.  | red |
Circle the set that has **less**.  | blue |

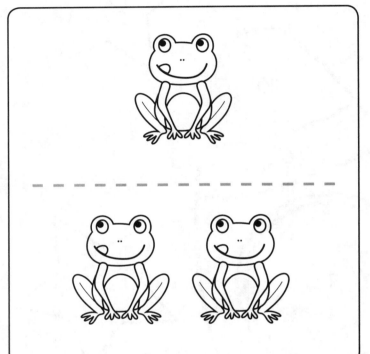

# Comparing Sets

Circle the set that has **more**. | green |
Circle the set that has **less**. | yellow |

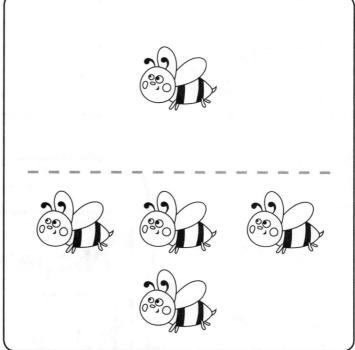

# Practice Your Phone Number

Print your phone number.
Practice calling your phone number.

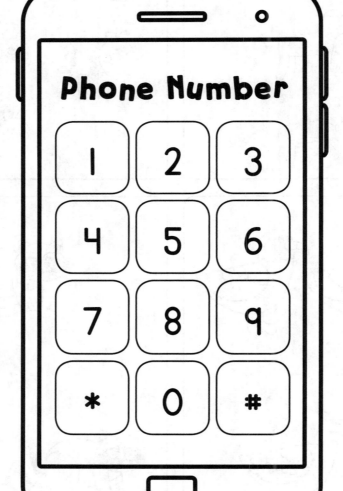

**Phone Number**

| 1 | 2 | 3 |
| 4 | 5 | 6 |
| 7 | 8 | 9 |
| * | 0 | # |

# More Learning Skills

# Matching Sets

Draw a line from each set of clothing to the appropriate weather.

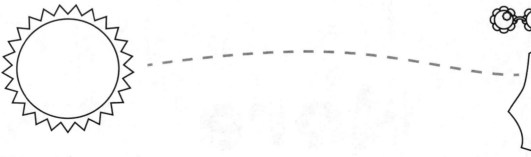

hot and sunny                                swimwear

cool and cloudy                            coat and mittens

raining                                        sweater

snowing                                  umbrella and boots

# Opposites

Draw a line to match the opposite pair.
Colour the pictures.

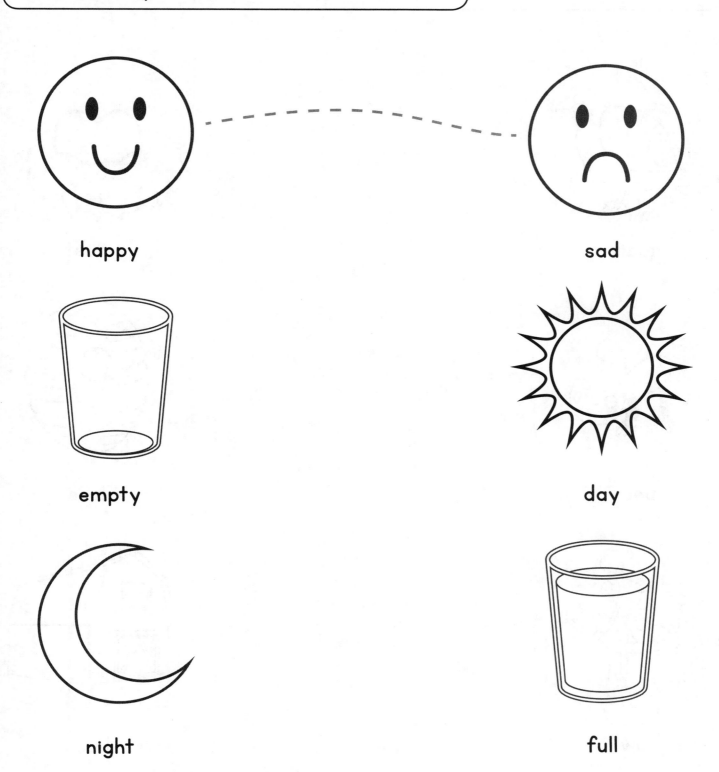

happy

sad

empty

day

night

full

# Left to Right

Help the animals get to their homes!
Trace the lines from left to right.

quail

left                    right

nest

bee

left                    right

hive

cow

left                    right

barn

# Top to Bottom

Help the spiders get down!
Trace the lines from top to bottom.

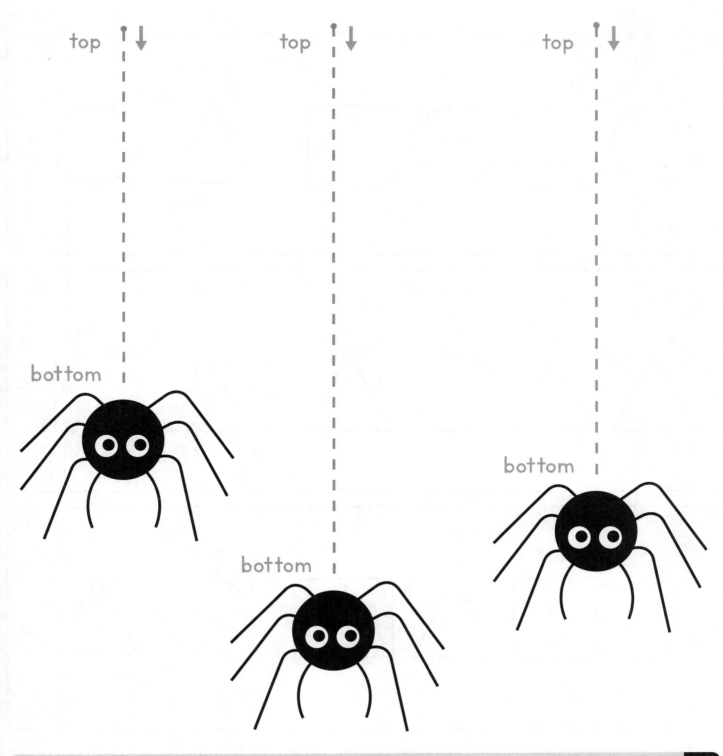

top

top

top

bottom

bottom

bottom

# Patterning Fun

Look at each pattern.
Colour the next shape in the pattern.

# Patterning Fun

Create your own colour patterns.

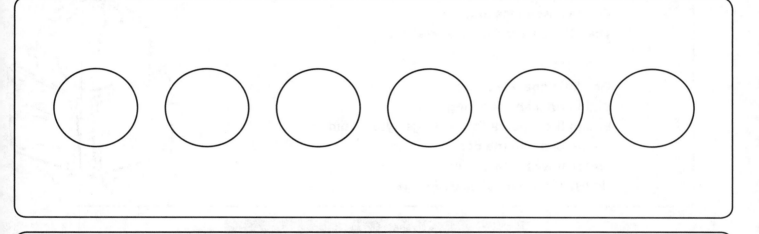

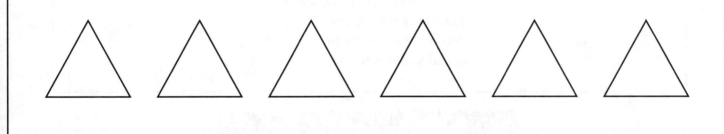

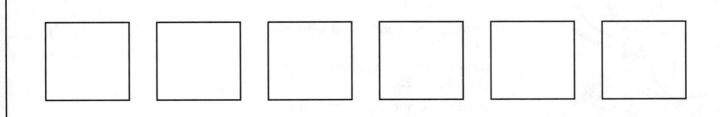

# Rhymes, Chants and Finger Plays

## Five Little Speckled Frogs

Five little speckled frogs,                                    *(hold up five fingers)*
Sitting on a speckled log,                                    *(sit down)*
Eating the most delicious bugs...yum, yum.    *(pretend to eat)*
One jumped into the pool                                    *(jump)*
Where it was nice and cool.
Then there were four speckled frogs.

*Continue until only one frog is left.*

One little speckled frog.
Sitting on a speckled log,
Eating the most delicious bugs...yum, yum.
He jumped into the pool
Where it was nice and cool.
Now there are no speckled frogs.

## Hickory, Dickory, Dock

Hickory, dickory, dock,
The mouse ran up the clock;
The clock struck one,
The mouse ran down;
Hickory, dickory, dock.

## Count to 100 Chant

Hooray! Hooray!
Count to 100 in different ways!

Count by 1's - its really fun!
1, 2, 3, 4, 5, .......

Count by 2's - I will count with you!
2, 4, 6, 8, 10, ......

Count by 5's - its easy if you try!
5, 10, 15, 20, 25, .....

Count by 10 and then start over again!
10, 20, 30, 40, .......

# Rhymes, Chants and Finger Plays

## Ten Fingers

| | |
|---|---|
| I have ten fingers | *(hold up both hands showing all ten fingers)* |
| And they all belong to me, | *(point to self )* |
| I can make them do things - | *(wiggle fingers)* |
| Would you like to see? | *(point to eyes)* |
| I can shut them up tight | *(make fists)* |
| I can open them wide | *(open hands and spread out fingers)* |
| I can put them together | *(clasp hands together)* |
| I can make them all hide | *(put hands behind back)* |
| I can make them jump high | *(hold hands over head )* |
| I can make them jump low | *(touch the floor with all ten fingers)* |
| I can fold them up quietly | *(fold hands in lap)* |
| And hold them just so. | |

## Who stole from the cookie jar

Who stole the cookie from the cookie jar?

_____ *(child's name)* **stole the cookie from the cookie jar.**

*(named child)* **Who me?**

*(other children)* **Ya you!**

*(named child)* **Couldn't be!**

*(other children)* **Then who?**

**Repeat above verse with the name of a new child.**

**Tip: The teacher may wish to have a cookie jar filled with student name cards.
Have a student pick a name card from the cookie jar to start the rhyme.**

## I'm a little teapot

| | |
|---|---|
| I'm a little teapot, short and stout | *(place one hand on hip to imitate a handle)* |
| | *(position other hand in the air to imitate a spout)* |
| Here is my handle, | |
| Here is my spout. | |
| When I get all steamed up | |
| Then I shout. | |
| Tip me over. | |
| And pour me out! | *(lean to the right to imitate pouring tea from the spout)* |

# Congratulations!
## Great Work!